the twilight gospel

THE SPIRITUAL
STEPHENIE MEY̶ ̶ ̶̶ ̶̶ ̶̶ ̶̶ ̶̶ ̶̶GA

DAVE ROBERTS

MONARCH
BOOKS

First published in the UK in 2009 by Monarch Books
(a publishing imprint of Lion Hudson plc),
Wilkinson House, Jordan Hill Road, Oxford OX2 8DR.
Tel: +44 (0)1865 302750 Fax: +44 (0)1865 302757
Email: monarch@lionhudson.com
www.lionhudson.com

ISBN: 978-1-85424-976-0

British Library Cataloguing Data
A catalogue record for this book is available from the British Library.

Printed and bound in the United States of America.

For all who are willing to go to Mars Hill (Acts 17).

CONTENTS

INTRODUCTION

You MAY PICK UP this book for any number of reasons.

Maybe you're a fan of the *Twilight* series and you're curious about the spiritual ideas that inform these stories.

It could be that you're a parent wanting to understand the books that have captured the imagination of your daughter or your son.

You might be a youth worker who wonders what has propelled the series to bestseller status and a 16 per cent share of all books sold in the USA in 2008. Perhaps you haven't read the books but you've seen one of the films and been drawn into the life of a sleepy town, with appalling weather, in Washington State.

The book you are about to read has a point of view. It is not a detached overview. It would be better to think of it as a respectful engagement. It will ask some hard questions of the values, ethics, wisdom and spiritual nuances of this saga. It will praise what is praiseworthy, but not flinch from questioning.

My own view of life is informed by mainstream Christian orthodoxy. Those who write about culture from within that perspective may sometimes be guilty of standing at opposite poles. Some only have to see the words 'sex' or 'occult' and go on the war path, denouncing the books in the broadest of terms and discouraging young people from reading them. Alternatively, others are mortified at a Christian perspective that is constantly 'against' culture and seek to find something of truth, beauty and hope in every corner. This second perspective will often be seeking what are called 'redemptive analogies'. These parables, pictures or metaphors within a storyline are seized upon as parallels to Christian truth and doorways to insight.

Tiptoeing boldly (if such a mixed metaphor is permitted) between these two perspectives is the book that you're about to read. It will seek a bigger perspective on the writing of Stephenie Meyer than one that only examines storylines about sexuality or occult activity.

But it will question whether this story really speaks to the rebellion associated with vampire imagery and mythology – or is, in fact, a hymn to more conventional values associated with individualism, consumerism and elitism.

The little boy in the story who was willing to blurt out that the emperor had no clothes is my guide. I'm not sure that the glamorous rebels of the *Twilight Saga* have any real hope for us. Is the 'rebel sell', which packages rebellion for mass consumption, at work in this modern-day romance?

I hope you enjoy our exploration.

DAVE ROBERTS

WWW.THINKCHRISTIAN.CO.UK

CHAPTER 1

THE USES OF

ENCHANTMENT

IN AN AGE WHEN the art of reading is thought to be in decline, the success of a book series with over 2,450 pages and a character count exceeding 3.5 million may be a surprise to some.

The appetite of readers old and young for romance, drama and the thrill of the long-running saga remains undimmed, however. The success of the *Harry Potter* series was just one indicator. The advent of the Internet has also made it possible to build strong fan cultures around niche television series such as *Buffy the Vampire Slayer* or *The West Wing*. At the heart of this fan culture activity is an identification with the characters in a storyline, and a desire to explore both the story and the point of view that lies behind it.

A young boy, Harry Potter, captured the imagination of many as he grew up with his audience. It seems fitting that the next mass-market mystical morality tale capturing the imaginations of children and young adults should feature a slightly awkward, self-conscious girl, teetering on the brink of womanhood.

While some may be tempted to dismiss these stories as *Mills & Boon* style romances for the young teen reader, at their heart they explore issues of identity, sexuality and spirituality. They reflect on material aspiration, prejudice and stereotyping, family breakdown, self-control and human dignity. They invoke the Bible and one of the characters speaks of the perspective of the Creator. They explore ancient myths and mystical practices that are entering the mainstream culture of the West.

Regardless of literary merit, the saga's cold, hard sales facts are staggering. The series is made up of five books. Four have been published, but an unpublished fragment – *Midnight Sun* – tells the story found in the original *Twilight* series from the perspective of Edward, the main male character in the books. The fragment is over 260 pages long and further fills in both the romantic and the spiritual roots of the story.

The series, which launched in 2005, has become a publishing phenomenon. With sales in excess of 70 million by 2009 and translations into 38 languages, the *Twilight Saga* has emerged as a strong competitor for hearts and minds alongside the *Harry Potter* series and the controversial *Da Vinci Code*. While originally published for 'young readers', the saga has attracted a much wider audience, including women looking for a different take on romantic fiction.

If you have found the 2,450-page mountain too hard a climb, or if you have read the series but would value a plot overview, here is a swift summary. Feel free to skip it if you know the books well.

TWILIGHT

Bella Swan has left Phoenix, Arizona to join her father in Forks, a small town in Washington State. She wants to allow her mother to travel with her new husband, whose job as a baseball player means many weeks away from home. Bella soon finds herself drawn to Edward Cullen, a mysterious figure admired by many women and despised by many men. Watching him, she concludes that there is more to Edward than meets the eye. She eventually discovers that he is a member of a vampire family who have vowed to drink only animal blood and to avoid attacking humans.

Bella and Edward stumble awkwardly into a relationship that they both desire but don't know how to initiate. Complications arise when they encounter another vampire group, whose 'tracker' James becomes bent on consuming Bella. The Cullen family are quick to defend her and eventually the marauding James is dispatched, despite having come very close to killing Bella. Her injuries are presented as the result of an accident in the hotel where she had been staying with Alice and Jasper, two other members of the Cullen family. Given Bella's notorious clumsiness, this is no surprise to anyone, and their cover story is accepted.

NEW MOON

Edward, despite his overpowering love for Bella, or perhaps because of that love, decides that the Cullen family must leave Forks so that the threat to her from other vampires, or Cullen family members who experience a brief lapse of control, is diminished. Bella is profoundly depressed but begins to return to emotional stability when she renews her friendship with Jacob Black, who is part of a local Native American tribe.

The plot twists and turns when Bella decides to jump from a high cliff into the sea. For her it is simply a slightly foolish but thrilling escapade – but it puts her in danger of drowning. It triggers the return of the Cullen family because they come to believe that Bella has died. Edward, filled with anguish, goes to Italy to provoke the Volturi, a form of vampire royalty, to kill him. He teeters on the brink of exposing the vampire presence in the city in order to persuade them to capture and eliminate him. The fateful moment passes, however, when Bella arrives on the scene. They are allowed to leave on the condition that Bella be turned into a vampire in the near future.

ECLIPSE

The Cullen family are increasingly aware that they have unfinished business with Victoria, the companion and lover of James, who had been killed and cremated following his attempt to kill Bella and drink her blood. Victoria is creating an army of 'newborn' vampires in order to wage a war with the Cullen clan and kill Bella. There are also significant romantic tensions as Bella seeks to come to terms with her feelings for both Jacob and Edward.

The werewolves and the vampires find common cause in opposing Victoria and are triumphant in the battle. Bella chooses Edward and agrees to marry him.

BREAKING DAWN

Bella and Edward marry but have to cut short their honeymoon because it's clear that Bella is pregnant and that the child is growing at an extraordinary rate. She comes close to death while giving birth but her life is saved when Edward initiates her as a vampire.

The new child, Renesmee, is mistaken by a vampire from another tribe for an 'immortal child'. The Volturi travel to Forks to punish this violation of vampire law. Many vampires travel to speak on behalf of the Cullen family and to protest that the child is not a destructive immortal and shows characteristics of humanity. Several of them train Bella to use the latent psychic skills that she has displayed throughout the story. Her use of these utterly thwarts the Volturi and they leave, declaring that no crime has been committed.

MIDNIGHT SUN

With respect to the already established plot, this unpublished storyline, written from the perspective of Edward and describing his initial encounters with Bella, adds little to the story. It does significantly deepen the characters of several of the main players. Edward is attracted by goodness and finds that being around it mellows him. His access to the thought life of several key characters was already a part of the dialogue in all of the books and is filled out further here, but not always in a way that casts these characters in a very good light.

Many will perhaps read these books and barely remember them. They will be the books of the month, literally and emotionally. But some will look upon them as a window on the world. Bella's emotions regarding her awkwardness will ring true for them. The astonishing intensity of first sexual experiences and the tentative discovery of trust at a profound level will seep out of the pages and into the thought patterns of many readers.

Learning from stories is an ancient aspect of our culture. Two thousand years ago Jesus held large crowds spellbound as he painted rich word-pictures with his parables and proverbs. As we encounter the stories that make up the *Twilight Saga* we will want to be aware, as Jesus was, that some will hear the story and hardly understand it, but others will deeply internalize the things that they hear.

Think for a moment of Jesus' story of the Prodigal Son, which Edward ruefully mentions upon his return from exile. (He had sought to protect Bella from vampire attack by being away from her.) Jesus draws the crowd into the emotional drama of the story as he recounts the ungrateful demands of the errant son. The extent of his downfall is made clear when we discover that he is feeding pigs. The depth of the father's mercy is planted as an idea in the imagination of the hearer as he or she pictures the father running to extend mercy, and to signal to the local population his protection of the son they had every reason to despise. The willingness of the father to forgive is clear, but the idea arises from the story rather than any explicit mention of the word. It is an example of skilful storytelling.

The skilful storyteller evokes emotion and encourages empathy with the characters. Many readers will feel as if they are spectators, hovering in the background of the dialogue that they read or the story they hear. They will picture the scenes as they play out on a backdrop in their imagination. This powerful connection with the emotions of a story will often connect people with a religion, a philosophy or a point of view.

Fiction, obviously, has power. But how much? Those who say that stories such as the *Twilight Saga* 'make' people undertake explorations of sexuality or the occult are overstating the case. Stories do not 'make' anybody do anything. They introduce the possibility and excite the imagination: that is all. By the same token, those who would say that these are merely stories and that people will not internalize the value systems they find in the saga may also be suffering from a form of cultural myopia. Some people will take up the possibilities that they find in the story and act them out in their own lives. Stories bring ideas to life.

As we journey into the *Twilight* lands around Seattle, where our story is set, let us bear in mind that there will be many other explorers. Some will be walking in Bella's shoes, deeply identified with her emotional vulnerability and her questions over her own character and motivations. Others will be fascinated by the vampire mythology, with its rebellion against the moral norms of society. They will be drawn into the struggles of those vampires who are reluctant to embrace their killing-machine destiny and hang on to shreds of humanity in the hope of redemption or as an antidote to guilt.

Some will simply be quietly thrilled with the erotic subtext that runs through all four books. Many are not the least bit interested in direct depictions of the sexual act but are happy to get lost in the erotic world of discovery that the young virgin and the 104-year-old man (who doesn't seem to have had a girlfriend since he was 18, if at all) embark upon.

Just as there is no typical *Twilight* reader, so there is no one message. The story has many layers, some of which we are going to explore. It weaves together ideas about material consumption, sexuality, spirituality, personal psychic power, self-image, friendship and social networks, the glamour of rebellion, folklore and even tribal conflict. No wonder it is potent stuff.

But in what sense, if any, is it true? I live my life according to a magnificent narrative handed down through the millennia by the apostles and prophets of the religion that honours God, his Son Jesus and his emissary to us today, the Holy Spirit. The *Twilight Saga* does not purport to be 'truth' but many will feel that it contains truth about their life. To determine what is true and praiseworthy, I will be examining the ideas at the heart of the *Twilight Saga* in the light of the ideas at the heart of the Christian faith.

Examining popular culture through the eyes of Christian thought can sometimes be a painful process, which is why many Christians choose to turn their backs on that culture. It's painful when the foundation we stand on is fear. Fear of what that culture might do to us. Fear of those who create that culture. Fear of what stain it might leave on our hearts or our minds. But I am not writing from a place of fear. I have no desire to plant seeds of fear in the lives of anyone who reads this book.

I want to write from a place of wisdom – not my own, but rather the wisdom I find throughout the pages of the Hebrew/Christian scriptures. In critiquing other worldviews, I desire to help people understand and respond and make good choices. I don't want to tell them what to believe about contemporary vampire culture! I do want to hold up the ideas in the *Twilight Saga* to scrutiny, and help the reader to ask good, penetrating questions about those ideas.

In the book of Revelation, Jesus addresses the seven churches of Asia Minor, calling them to account for their behaviour. He speaks very well of two of them and affirms something positive about every one of the other five. But he also says, 'this I have against you'. As you read on you'll discover that I affirm some of the story threads in the *Twilight Saga*. You'll also discover very searching questions. They are offered in the spirit of the approach that Jesus took with the errant churches.

You and I are not Jesus and the *Twilight Saga* is not a church (although the www.twilightsaga.com website does have 183,000 members at the time of writing). The *Twilight Saga* does not affirm mainstream orthodox Christianity in its storylines or dialogue. But it does contain elements of what is good and wholesome. For instance, in Carlisle Cullen we find a man of peace. Bella is almost painfully humble, as well as being willing to sacrifice her life for others. Charlie Swan loves his daughter. Angela Weber personifies a quiet goodness. Esme Carlisle has the instinctive protective love of a mother, but towards children who are not her own. As you wander the *Twilight* lands, you'll find grace, beauty and truth in the midst of moral complexity and spiritual promiscuity.

I want to acknowledge wisdom where we find it in the story, and to respect the fine storyteller who brings us the tale. We should be willing to stand in the shoes of other readers who come to this story with different expectations, backgrounds and experiences. But as we seek to understand why the story touches them, I hope we will also be willing to question and refute, and perhaps, when necessary, say 'this I have against you'.

But first we need to go to Transylvania.

CHAPTER 2

THE FEAR

OF THE DEAD

FINDING A STEREOTYPICAL VAMPIRE is quite hard work. The vampires of Forks, Washington, are both typical of the genre and completely untypical. But where on earth did the idea arise of dead creatures, endowed with immortality and passing on their abilities with a venomous bite?

Creatures who escape from the grave and attack the living in order to satisfy their need for blood can be traced to the folklore of nations on all five continents. In a typical myth the creature might rise from the grave and attack innocent local people, or wreak revenge on enemies from his or her human existence. The blood-crazed killer then returns to the grave to hide until the next opportunity to pillage and murder.

In such stories, when the local community had absolved the living of the blame for a murder, their thoughts would turn to the graveyard. In some cultures the suspected vampire would be exhumed and the head cut off to prevent further gruesome attacks. As an insurance policy a giant stake would be driven through their bodies. The corpses of those suspected of being vampires might have their clothes nailed to the inside of the coffin to further hinder the possibility of escape. According to the Bible, there is a real possibility of spotting the previously deceased. King Saul was castigated for consulting with the Witch of Endor. The disciples witnessed Jesus in conversation with Moses and Elijah on the Mount of Transfiguration. Jesus returned from the dead, was identified by his disciples, and was later seen by up to 500 witnesses. Shortly after his death, the bodies of the saints were said to have risen from the dead and been sighted all around Jerusalem.

While the Bible hints that another type of human-like creature might have inhabited the Earth at one time – the Nephilim – it seems to suggest that they were angelic beings and that their consorting with the women of the Earth earned the displeasure of God.

The vampire myth of the previously human, who returns after death to attack the living, would seem to have no precedent in the classical scriptures of the Jewish, Christian and Islamic faiths, however. Such stories are quite widespread, but only in folklore and ancient fables. There is no credible scientific or archaeological evidence for vampires. Exhumations that purported to discover bodies bloated with blood were often poorly decomposed bodies buried in poor soil. Blood around the mouth was likely the result of pneumonic illness, including the plague.

Any story that contains a supernatural element will always need to be accepted through the lens of faith. Biblical depictions of the undead simply suggest that people have returned in a recognizable human form and interacted with those still conventionally alive. In the context of other biblical accounts of the miraculous, these seem less unlikely – consider that the Bible also describes the supernatural creation of the universe, Christ's resurrection from the dead and a wide spectrum of inexplicable miracles involving healing power (Jesus), future knowledge (choose your prophet), insight into other people's thoughts (Jesus) and miraculous transportation (the disciple Phillip). Once you accept the premise that God interacts with the created order and that conventional cause-and-effect may be laid aside as he undertakes his work, then the appearance of the deceased does not seem to break the boundaries of the possible. But the undead in the Christian scriptures simply impart their wisdom and go.

No doubt those of our forebears who believed that a ghastly murder should be attributed to the undead had their reasons. Such mythology may have created a smokescreen to hide the real intent and identity of those who would seek to kill for their own gain. Fabricating stories of the supernatural has frequently been a means of influence or financial advantage. But those seeking concrete evidence of the murderous activities of the previously dead will search in vain.

Strangely enough, in Britain things vampiric took a new turn following the advent of the Sunday school movement. While it brought huge benefit to many by helping them learn to read the biblical stories for themselves, it was also a means by which the newly literate could explore less edifying material. Vampire tales soon became a reading staple for many, no longer the stuff of oral tradition or folklore, but available in the high street for a penny. These 'penny dreadfuls' frequently depicted humans who had become vampires.

The vampire myth before the Middle Ages had often centred around demonic, *other-worldly* creatures who attacked humans in order to drink their blood. As the myths developed, the vampire was often thought to be an unbaptized child, or the child of unmarried persons, or simply someone who had been spectacularly evil during their life. Some believed that the body could not release the spirit to its home in the afterlife until it had fully decomposed and that these earth-shackled spirits rose to exact revenge for problems encountered in their human lives.

Four vampire figures came to dominate the popular imagination after the rise of cheap printing and greater literacy. These literary vampires would add new potency to the ancient mythology. They represented a veritable host of vampire archetypes and elements of them all creep into the *Twilight* narrative.

Dr Poldari, an associate of the famed poet Lord Byron, helped pioneer the modern vampire story by taking the structure of one of Byron's ghost stories and embellishing it with vampire folklore in a book entitled *The Vampyre*. His vampire, Lord Ruthven, preys on his innocent friends, who are drawn into his circle of influence through his charming, aristocratic manner. The image of the vampire at home in smart society was an innovation, and a departure from popular folklore. The socially polished vampire with the beautiful face also forms a part of the *Twilight* story: Edward marvels at his own ability to both dazzle and frighten the ordinary mortals amongst whom he lives.

The next innovation in the vampire genre was James Malcolm Rymer's long-running *Varney the Vampyre* series. Varney is an ugly vampire, whose exploits extend to 237 chapters. His gaunt frame is forever on the run from the angry mob who wish to punish him for his death sprees. The Cullen family's angst over their vampire destiny also reflects the introduction by Rymer in the Varney stories of a note of despair and a craving for love and friendship. Varney tells the priest that he thought 'that I had steeled my heart against all gentle impulses... but it is not so'. Eventually Varney can handle it no longer and takes himself off to Mount Vesuvius to sacrifice himself to the fire and end his own reign of terror.

Sheridan Le Fanu developed the genre further with his book *Carmilla*. Here, for the first time, is a female literary vampire. The barely masked sexual undertones of the books by Poldari and Rymer now take a new direction with a female vampire who preys on other females and speaks to them in the language of ownership: 'you are mine, you shall be mine, you and I are one forever.'

Much of the story portrays Carmilla as young and

innocent, and the reader is invited to sympathize with her plight. Le Fanu also begins to dismantle some of the normal religious structure that surrounded vampire mythology and has his heroines buying charms and crosses without effect, despite their powerful influence in other vampire myth accounts. Bella professes shock when she finds a massive cross inside the Cullen house, but Edward assures her that its power over vampires has been exaggerated.

Bram Stoker's *Dracula* produced perhaps the most iconic and well-known symbol of vampirism. Stoker was not scared to reach back and introduce folkloric elements or ancient demon stories into his fiction. But they were surrounded with the symbolism of the modern day. Mechanical music-players, characters using shorthand and blood transfusions all played their part in the Dracula narrative. Stoker's vampires were likely to explode into dust when exposed to sunlight, but the vampires of Forks, Washington merely glisten and sparkle. The vampire clans of the *Twilight* series have no need of sleep and are not found in coffins or earthly graves – another variation on the vampire canon.

The mythology continued to grow, and the possibility of creating new vampires by biting, but not killing, became a staple of vampire literature. Vampires had been thought to be undead spirits or demons sent by the devil. But Eastern European variants of the vampire story introduced the idea that to be bitten by a vampire meant that you too got to join the undead.

Two other major blockbusters have catapulted vampires into a higher profile. New Orleans-based writer Anne Rice has written a variety of vampire novels that attracted literary acclaim and were turned into films such as *Interview with a Vampire*, starring Tom Cruise. Rice blurred the sexuality of her vampires, moving away from the sexually voracious female vampire and the rapacious male vampire towards more androgynous, glamorous figures who were attractive because of their status as forbidden outsiders, as well as their physical appeal.

But books and films are essentially short-term experiences. The advent of *Buffy the Vampire Slayer* was not the first vampire-orientated TV series, but it was the first to go to seven separate seasons. Now you could re-enter that world every week. If you had cable TV you could view the same episode several times over, if you hadn't already bought the boxed DVD set.

Here too we find conflicted vampires, Angel and Spike, ill at ease with a conventional vampire job description and seen as good guys by the audience because they possess a 'soul' and forsake the gratification of blood.

Large numbers of fans contributed to the thought patterns and ideas that lay behind the *Buffy* story, because Joss Whedon, one of the key writers of the series, was willing to engage with the fan base via the Internet and to let that fan base discuss the stories, express their feelings about the characters and create their own scripts based on key figures in the storyline. In some ways it was unimportant whether vampirism was a reality. It was a story that you could discuss and own.

Writing in *The Lure of The Vampire*, Milly Williamson argues that vampire mythology has become one of the places where people go to explore morality in the absence of a willingness to embrace the truth claims of conventional religion. The rise of the sympathetic vampire gives people a way of discussing what it means to try to be imperfectly good. (Jesus' twelve disciples were imperfectly good, too, but many never get close enough to a thoughtful expression of Christianity to explore what that might mean.)

Into this arena emerged the *Twilight* series. As the saga-hungry lamented the end of the Harry Potter epic, so a new story of the fantastical made its appearance. Neither story was the first to serialize an epic theme.

C. S. Lewis, writing in the 1950s, had quite deliberately woven elements of the fantastic into his *Chronicles of Narnia*, but placed a Christ-like figure, Aslan, at the heart of the story. Once you knew that Aslan's life was a metaphor for Christ's work, then you could reinterpret the story in that light, should you so choose.

Tolkien took the structures of Scandinavian myth and wove some of his Roman Catholic sensibilities into the storyline. Although many would feel that *The Lord of the Rings* conveyed a basic morality sympathetic to Christian ideals, for others it was simply the start of a journey into a genre of epic literature that mixed the supernatural and the mundane, the heroic and the violent.

There are other pretenders to the meaningful-myth throne. Phillip Pullman sailed into the imagination of many a child via his *Dark Materials* series. It too has a spiritual agenda. Pullman despises the Christian archetypes of C. S. Lewis, and is determined to confront head-on the story narratives of Christianity and its engagement with history during the last 2,000 years. His rather crude attacks on the church are far from new. Pullman is not saying anything that Christians themselves have not said. Within Christian traditions that critiqued militarism, nationalism and any kind of state religion,

Pullman's critique of historical Popes and leading Protestant figures such as John Knox and John Calvin would not have been hailed as a startling piece of original thought. But the compellingly readable package it comes in, with its promotion of the idea of personal 'daemons' and its underlying bitterness towards Christianity, has meant that it has attracted widespread admiration.

Fiction with occult themes can be hugely popular around the world. With large sections of the population professing nominal attachment to some kind of conventional Christianity, but mixing that cheerfully with astrology, fortune-telling, ouija boards and spiritualism, Feng Shui and reiki healing, yoga and palm-reading, the popular imagination does not revolt against storylines that convey supernatural themes and moral exploration.

If people only broadly articulate a belief in God, but have little engagement with the life of Christ or the moral wisdom of the Old and New Testaments, they will often embrace non-demanding forms of the supernatural which seem to have an immediate benefit in terms of healing or personal empowerment. Literature which explores spiritual realities, creates fantastical mythological backgrounds and reflects on human frailty whilst pushing away extreme evil, will appeal simply at the level of escapist literature, but may – and this is a major aspect of its appeal – also resonate with the realities of the reader's life.

So what has the *Twilight Saga* brought to the vampires' table?

It has both embraced and set aside aspects of the conventional vampire genre. Like *Buffy*, it is set in the present. While the Cullen vampires are highly fashionable, they do not fit into a stylized 'black clothing and lace' vampire stereotype. Edward sarcastically reminds Bella that he doesn't have the vampire fangs of popular mythology, but Stephenie Meyer has placed her characters firmly within the vampire canon by ensuring that they avoid the sun by living in the darkness or in a climate where there is very little sunlight.

Shrewdly, Meyer creates a moral universe for her vampire clans, which adds greatly to the novels' power and appeal. In the centre stand the Volturi, who have no compunction about seducing humans and drinking their blood as long as everything is discreet and the normal life of society remains undisturbed. They are not in a hurry to create new vampires. They are ruled over by three ancients, Aro, Caius and Marcus, who, together with their ruthless psychic bodyguards, help maintain order amongst vampires worldwide.

The Volturi are sometimes called into action to curb the behaviour of renegade vampires who are creating armies of the 'newborn' who slaughter without compunction and attack both humans and other vampires. This aspect of vampire morality intrudes into the *Twilight Saga* when a vampire called Victoria creates dozens of vampires who embark on a reign of terror around Seattle. Victoria enlists their help in her quest for revenge for the death of her lover and companion James (who was killed by the Cullens after he attacked Bella). This army is decimated by the Cullens and the werewolves, who unite to defeat them.

Providing a counterpoint to both the Volturi and Victoria is Dr Carlisle Cullen. He has taken a conscious decision to avoid taking human life, and confines his vampiric activity to animals, many of which would be hunted by conventional humans. He has created a number of vampires to be his companions and schooled them in the ways of peace and co-existence. He is scrupulous about only initiating those who were going to die anyway and has sought to do away with old enmities by initiating peace with a nearby Native American tribe whose young men have the ability to phase into the shape of a werewolf. The vampires stay away from their land and agree not to create new vampires. Dr Cullen has trained himself so well that he is able to work as a conventional doctor without succumbing to the urge to attack his patients, especially when they have wounds that he is required to work on.

Not all his foster children find it quite so easy. Edward has cultivated a great deal of self-control over the decades but is undone by the sheer overpowering appeal of Bella (as a potential meal) and has to exercise the most extreme caution. During his adolescent years of rebellion Edward had simply targeted violent killers and so applied a vigilante logic to his behaviour.

Jasper, his foster brother and the companion of the in-house Cullen psychic Alice, was previously part of a highly destructive group of vampires and still fights to control his urges with respect to humans. His barely-contained frenzy when Bella cuts her finger at a birthday party in her honour at the Cullen house, is the catalyst for Edward's decision to move the Cullen family away and allow Bella to avoid the risks associated with her friendship with vampires.

The other Cullen vampires are not immune to the appeal of human blood, but seem to be more in control of their reactions. One of them, Rosalie, is deeply unhappy that she is a vampire, and all of them would seize the chance to be human again if such a thing was possible.

Stephenie Meyer does not portray the Cullens as a perfect family. In the unpublished *Midnight Sun* manuscript, Edward reveals the murderous intent of Jasper, Rosalie and Emmett when they think that his interaction with Bella will expose their secret within the Forks community. They may have turned from a life of terror and human bloodletting, but unlike Dr Cullen and his wife Esme, who emerge throughout all five books as highly pacifistic, they are pragmatic about relaxing the rules in extreme circumstances. Emmett also admits to the occasional unpremeditated lapse and Rosalie was permitted to go back and kill those who had raped her and left her for dead.

Other vampires in their circle who have also turned their back on human killing do not have the same basic revulsion about killing humans that has helped motivate the Cullen family. The Denali coven comprises three women, one of whom, Tanya, has made it very clear to Edward that she would like a relationship with him: he, however, has already begun to fall under Bella's spell. Edward suggests in *Midnight Sun* that Tanya and her friends enjoy sex so much that they have settled down and avoided killing humans so they can have as much opportunity as possible to indulge their other hungers.

So we are presented with a group of heroes who

are essentially good, but morally complex and sometimes frail as they seek to find their way in the world. Many readers will not be attracted to a perfect hero. (Christian readers will be aware that few figures in the Bible except Jesus emerge as perfect heroes.)

Stephenie Meyer does not ask us to believe that vampires are real. She invites us to visit a mythical world, albeit one with a strong overlap to our own. As she explores the differences between the good, the bad and the downright evil vampires, she encourages us to look more searchingly at love and life, death and conflict, teen angst and identity, religion and spirituality.

So much for the vampires. What of the human at the core of the story?

⇜

CHAPTER 3

YOU'VE GOT TO BE

PERFECT

THERE IS AN OLD PROVERB about walking a mile in someone else's shoes. The problem with taking a walk in Bella's shoes is this: if your life were to imitate hers, you would spend a lot of time falling over. If there is one dominant motif in the *Twilight Saga*, over and beyond that of the love between Edward and Bella, it is Bella's sheer clumsiness. The three key males in the storyline, Edward Cullen, Jacob Black and Charlie Swan (her dad), spend much of the time responding to this or worrying about what she is going to do next.

BELLA'S CLUMSINESS

It is a key aspect of Bella's sense of self-worth and identity and is core to our understanding of her attitudes throughout the story. She believes she attracts accidents like a magnet. What is the evidence for this?

Bella has poor hand–eye coordination and spends a lot of her sports lessons accidentally hitting the other pupils with volleyballs, badminton rackets and the like.

She resolutely refuses to believe that she could have any skill at dancing. She studiously avoids the dance at school for that reason and is unhappy about having to dance at the prom, until Edward comes to her rescue and essentially relieves her of the responsibility of having her feet on the ground.

By her own estimation, she falls down a lot. She is deeply embarrassed about stumbling and dropping her books following one of her early encounters with Edward. She drops a key in a puddle, drops a camera and crashes the bike that Jacob has repaired for her – twice. She drops the plate in the family kitchen and precipitates Edward's departure with a paper cut that unleashes bloodlust amongst the vampires (particularly Jasper). She clings to her dad on the wedding day and implores him: 'Don't let me fall, Dad.'

Her low sense of self-esteem emerges time and time again. She describes her handwriting as a 'clumsy scrawl'. The time she spends living with the Cullens when she is being hunted by the predatory vampire Victoria only compounds her sense of awkwardness. She notes: 'Hanging out with no one but extremely dextrous people all the time was giving me a complex.'

Once she has assumed her new identity as a vampire, her problems with awkwardness end. She develops a better sense of equilibrium and hears herself described as graceful, for probably the first time ever. After eighteen years of what she considered to be mediocrity, she now sees herself as a beautiful and competent woman.

WHAT DOES THE AWKWARDNESS MEAN FOR BELLA?

She is deeply conscious of her propensity to blush and is also reluctant to touch things in case she breaks them. She uses the language of self-deprecation on several occasions and calls herself an 'accident-prone klutz'.

This clumsiness produces a form of self-loathing in her insecure mind. She believes that her lack of grace means that she isn't interesting. As far as she's concerned, she is not good enough for Edward, partly because his physical grace and beauty only serve to expose her clumsiness.

The depth of her negativity is captured in her comment to Edward that she is 'so clumsy I am almost disabled'. To her way of thinking, her mind doesn't work right, and this makes her a freak. She tells herself that there is something wrong with her brain.

It is this lack of self-confidence that has kept Bella on the social sidelines. Reluctant to dance, concerned about clumsiness in front of a date, unaware of her own attractiveness and caught up in a vicious cycle of comparison to others, Bella has expended her energies on schoolwork and on looking after her mother, and more latterly her father.

WHAT IS THE IMPORTANCE OF THIS PART OF THE STORYLINE?

This is a very important aspect of the overall story and helps us to understand the resonance of the entire series for a significant part of its female readership. Adolescent awkwardness is a well-observed phenomenon amongst those who care for the physical and emotional health of teenagers. Sutton Hamilton comments:

Many school-age children struggle with motor skills that their peers have long mastered. Such children, often described as 'clumsy', may have difficulties with writing and skills such as dressing and eating unassisted. Often the diagnosis of clumsiness in children is missed as both parents and the child's physician may not recognize the child's coordination problems as a significant medical concern. Research for the last 20 years has shown that these coordination problems tend to persist, rather than resolve, through adolescence and adulthood.

In 1975, Dr. S. S. Gubbay coined the term 'clumsy child syndrome' to describe children of normal intelligence and without identifiable medical or neurological conditions who possess difficulties in coordination that interfere with their academic performance and/or socialization. The term 'clumsy child syndrome' has been replaced by the term 'Developmental Coordination Disorder' (DCD), but the diagnostic criteria have remained essentially the same.

Approximately 6 per cent of school-age children suffer from significant clumsiness, with boys more commonly affected than girls. The diagnosis is usually made between the ages of six and twelve, rarely before age five. The exact cause of clumsiness remains unknown.

SUTTON HAMILTON, 'EVALUATION OF THE CLUMSY CHILD', PEDIATRICS FOR PARENTS

The growing body must learn new movements and new skills. The literature that surrounds the academic study of adolescent clumsiness suggests that depression and poor self-image can often be related problems. The impact of poor physical skills can be significant, particularly during this time of life when a person is at their most self-conscious.

WHAT DOES IT MEAN FOR THE READER?

It is a very broad generalization, but even a short trip around the Internet, in the company of Google, in search of comment on the *Twilight* series, will turn up cynical teenagers moaning about Stephenie Meyer's reduction of vampirism to a bad habit that can be kicked with enough willpower. These same readers want to distance themselves from what they perceive to be a dilution of the genre and dismiss the books as the literary diet of another social grouping, held by them in low esteem. This dismissal of Meyer's romantic fiction is linked to the assumption that many of the readers come from the part of youth culture that is identified by the title 'Emo'. They are not quite 'Goths', their brooding cultural cousins, but are known for the introspection that marks the music that they identify with. The idea that Bella would appeal to a social group marked by intelligence and introspection is not a far-fetched one. Emo girls will not view themselves as the glamour girls of their high school and may suffer clumsiness issues and a dislike of sport similar to Bella's.

The readers may therefore identify with the vulnerability of Bella. They emotionally connect with the story because she is not a perfectly accomplished heroine, and her daily experiences ring true for many of the readers.

There are any number of ways in which people move past this stage in their life. They may simply learn new habits of movement and coordination and grow out of the clumsiness. They may spend time with parents, friends or teachers concentrating on a particular skill so that they can unlearn past patterns and move on.

None of them will have the option given to Bella. They cannot go to their high-school nurse and ask for some of that nice 'vampire venom' that miraculously creates beauty and physical grace in everyone it touches.

Bella's clumsiness is very real. The solution found in *Twilight* (first, become a vampire) is deeply unsatisfactory and brings a real tension for the reader who identifies with Bella's wounded emotions in this area.

BELLA'S SELF-IMAGE AND HER VIEW OF BEAUTY

Bella shows a degree of detachment when it comes to clothing, preferring her jeans and T-shirt. She is also ambivalent about the trappings of wealth that she encounters in the palatial Cullen mansion. One cannot portray her as a one-dimensional consumer of the American dream. But the chink in her armour is her constant reference to beauty in her descriptions of others.

It is implicit for many that to possess great beauty will be the key to establishing a relationship with a beautiful member of the opposite sex. It may be a myth, but it is very strongly held, especially by teenagers.

Bella's perception of Edward's beauty is closely tied to her desire for him, which we examine in Chapter 5, 'Sex and the Country'. In the present chapter we will concentrate on what some call the 'looks-based' view of beauty that is a constant theme in Bella's thought patterns.

The pattern begins to emerge when she first encounters the Cullens, whom she describes as inhumanly beautiful. She is arrested by their straight, perfect, angular faces, which to her appear to be almost angelic. She regards Edward's face as a complete distraction and has to fight the temptation to simply ogle him.

She is clearly an advocate of the 'muscled, six-pack abs' school of male physique and is aroused by Edward's perfectly muscled chest. Such is his perfection that in her view, 'There was nothing about him that could be improved on'.

In her mind she is not in the same league as Edward and his family. More than once she reflects that he looks like a male model but that she does not have the attributes to be a female model. His beauty pierces her with sadness and she reflects that there is no 'way this god-like creature could be meant for me'.

While she is attracted to Edward, she uses the beauty of others as a comparison point. Carlisle Cullen has an outrageous perfection about him. Rosalie she perceives as breath-taking and feels pity for every other girl in the room when faced with Rosalie's gloriously beautiful body and exquisite face. Bella is quite convinced that she could not compete with her beauty, which is so marked that it makes her want to cry. (Jacob is by no means as convinced and echoes a common cultural reservation over the merchandising of a culturally conditioned beauty when he calls Rosalie an 'ice-cold Barbie'.)

When the immortal beauty of the Cullens becomes a reality for Bella herself, she can hardly recognize the transformed person, noting what she regards as a familiar flaw in her lips as the proof that it's still her despite the change. She has become 'indisputably beautiful, every bit as beautiful as Alice or Esme'. Despite her previous awkwardness, she is 'fluid even in stillness'. She jokes with Edward about her new-found status and his ongoing inability to read her mind, and says to herself as much as to him, 'at least I'm pretty'. The duckling has indeed become a swan. Moreover, the mortal has become an immortal – a potent, and very old, storyline.

THE POISON PILL

The *Twilight Saga* provokes us to think about God, good and evil, conflict resolution, prejudice and division, teen awkwardness and the nature of romantic love. Much of it is positive and attractive.

But actually the series can have a far more insidious effect because of its relative innocence and the vulnerability of its characters. Even as we read the books, we recoil from the shallow sexual fantasies of Mike Newton, the jealous control-freakery of Rosalie or the pure evil of the murderous James and Victoria.

So when the innocent character with whom we emotionally connect espouses a particular set of values, we are less likely to react against them. The poison pill at the heart of these books is the legitimization of the 'beauty myth' as a consequence of Bella's constant references to beauty throughout the entire series. There is no critical distance in her comments. She is not offering a critique of the mindset: it is second nature to her. For Bella, beauty is a goal to be hankered for.

Selling the 'beauty myth' back to an audience already buffeted by its demands is, frankly, pernicious. The social psychologist Karen Dill, who wrote a frequently cited academic paper on the connection between video games and violence, makes the following observations in *How Fantasy Becomes Reality* (Oxford University Press, 2009):

- Beauty contest participants are 25 per cent smaller, weight wise, than the average woman. We are asked to aspire to the unreal.
- A study by Kristen Harrison into television portrayal of women noted that the ideal TV sizes for a woman were size 10 (breasts), size 2 (waist) and size 4 (hips). This combination is very rare in real life.
- Studies reveal pathological rates of body

dissatisfaction among women. These rates are often around 95 per cent. Most women in the West are uneasy, distressed or downright depressed about the way they look.

- The cultural conditioning starts young. Princess Jasmine, the female heroine of Disney's *Aladdin*, would be alarming if she were real. Her eyes are bigger than her waist. (Her overall presentation relies more on the *Playboy* view of femininity, espoused by those who drew her, than the reality of teenage physique).

- For many women, this on-screen exaggeration leads to a real-life sense of inadequacy and an obsession with trying to win an impossible game.

- Naomi Wolf, writer of *The Beauty Myth*, notes that the diet, cosmetics and cosmetic surgery industries are among the fastest growing in Western economies and generate in excess of $55 billion per annum.

- Dill's research indicates that a significant majority of female students would like not to have to do their hair and make-up every day, and would gladly step off the merry-go-round if they thought they could get away with it.

- The effects of this conditioning are, in Dill's view, deep and logic-defying. 'Our feelings of insecurity generated by mass media imagery are largely unconscious.'

If we were to ask what the basic tenets of the *Twilight* series were, and what its spiritual message was, we would hear some very unclear notes. We find loving families, compassionate people and (within certain limits) moral clarity. But we also find a wholehearted endorsement of the foundational values of Western humanism, where only the fittest flourish, free to consume material goods and each other's beautiful bodies.

DEFINING YOUR FRIENDSHIPS IN TERMS OF BEAUTY

Some of the more famous storytelling franchises such as *Star Wars* or *Star Trek* invest a great deal of energy in ensuring consistency within storylines. It's not uncommon, however, for a big cinema release of a popular book to diverge from the plotline and to create a new meaning for a scene or a character. The filming of the first book, *Twilight*, immediately threw up some problems.

In the original book, Bella and Edward are both keen to distance themselves from those that they regard as shallow. Lauren is regarded as fickle, bitchy and pretty. Jessica is an utter pragmatist whose affections shift from Edward to Mike Newton and back again over the course of both *Twilight* and *Midnight Sun*. Bella is more tolerant of the weaknesses of others while Edward silently fumes about most of his school friends – until, that is, his meandering through the thought lives of his fellow pupils introduces him to the steady goodness of Angela Weber. Bella also regards Angela as a steady friend, who doesn't need to be talking all the time and makes you unconditionally welcome.

So far, so good. A healthy awareness of shallow attitudes and a willingness to persevere with friendships seems like a positive combination. Less agreeably, both Edward and Bella are dismissive towards Eric. He is one of the people who initially makes Bella welcome, but she is wary of his friendship, mentally dismissing him as an overly helpful, chess-club type with poor hygiene. Edward is little better and files him away in his mental index as someone with poor hair and spots. Although Bella is an outsider, the new face in the school, and the Cullens have always perceived themselves as outsiders, they share the judgemental attitude of their classmates towards one who is universally regarded as an outsider.

This mental downgrading occurs again in Rosalie's dismissal of Bella as 'plain' and Edward's dismissal of Tyler as 'tediously average'.

The film-makers must have baulked. This was

not a film that wanted to engage with geek culture versus jock culture versus princess of the prom culture in the way that *The Breakfast Club* or *She's All That* or *Mean Girls* had done. Conventional Hollywood film-making for teens always wants beautiful people at the core of each shot. The ethereal beauty of the Cullen family is at the heart of both the books and the film, and especially the visual iconography surrounding the portrayal of Edward by Robert Pattinson. It was all going to jar a little if earlier scenes contained a 'spotty geek' like Eric. So he was made over as the college journalist with beautiful black hair, great taste in clothes and a defiantly metrosexual sensibility.

All in all, this becomes a no-win situation for both the film-makers and Stephenie Meyer. The film ducks the issue and changes the script to include a prettier character. Back in the books Stephenie Meyer is left with a kink in the goodness, tolerance and niceness scripting of both Bella and Edward. Bella is publicly civil to Eric and indeed steers him and Angela together for a dance that she is studiously avoiding, because as Edward notes, she is selfless and alert to the needs of others, but also because it solves her problem. She has an excuse, to do with her trip to Seattle, and a solution.

But, in the book, the pull of the beauty myth,

discussed above, shows its ugly face in the sadly hackneyed depiction of Eric in terms of his spots, his hair and his hobbies. The message is: if you're going to be good, be beautiful too. Beautiful people are only a problem when they are shallow and lack character.

Contrast the radical stance of Jesus, who saw, loved and sought out the marginal and the unlovely. He touched the leper when he healed him. This offended the religious people, who believed the leper to be ritually unclean. Jesus could have healed the leper from afar, but he chose to offer a signal of acceptance by reaching out his hand. There would be many other instances of this explicit compassion and inclusion. He entered the house of the diminutive tax collector Zacchaeus, which provoked great hostility amongst a crowd who might otherwise have welcomed Jesus to Jericho.

The echo of his life resounds beyond the Gospels. After Jesus' death and resurrection, the leaders of the young church in Jerusalem (which was predominantly Jewish) appointed deacons to ensure that the widows from Greek backgrounds were not neglected in the distribution of food. The biblical writer James castigates his readers, who were giving privileged positions in the seating arrangements of the church to the rich and powerful. Paul warns the Corinthians that their communion practices were marginalizing the less well-off. Commentators believe that the Corinthians were adopting the habits of the surrounding culture and slipping back into the Graeco-Roman meal patterns, where the rich and the favoured ate in the dining-rooms and others were pushed to the edges, the corridors and the gardens.

Jesus had provoked both his followers and his enemies by commenting on the spiritual faith of outsiders such as the devout centurion, the good Samaritan and the historical figure of Naaman the Leper who, several centuries previously, had been cured after bathing in the Jordan. To many in his audience this would have been an affront to their nationalist religious pride, and indeed, it sparked an attempt to kill Jesus in Nazareth.

The examples of the last three paragraphs are only a snapshot of the threads and strands in the life of Jesus that compel us away from an attitude that thinks of 'outsiders' and 'insiders' in the social sphere.

If we are to applaud the *Twilight Saga*, as we should, for believing that evil must be resisted and that goodness should be rewarded, we will also have to ask some hard questions about its understanding of beauty, its slavish admiration of perfection, and the nature of social exclusion. In recent years the fashion industry has had a hard time from critics who attack its predilection for impossibly slender models, arguing that the industry encourages anorexia and a poor self-image among those who long from the sidelines. Sadly, Stephenie Meyer worships the same idols.

We have to ask the questions because we believe that while popular fiction or popular film may not 'make' anybody do anything, the diet that we consume will have some impact on our emotional health and personal worldview if we have not rigorously examined its assumptions. What messages about beauty, self-image and personal contentment is the *Twilight Saga* giving to the emotionally vulnerable, often insecure, maybe not conventionally beautiful, adolescent audience that forms its core market?

Are they being offered a 'wish dream', an unobtainable life? Will reading these books provide a temporary escape from a disappointing reality, or could they in the long term actually deepen the despair for some, who are told once again that they must aspire to physical beauty if they are to gain the good things in life?

Which brings us to the role of the consumer queen, Alice.

CHAPTER 4

MAKE ME LIKE ALICE

IF THERE IS ONE CONSTANT POSITIVE in Bella's life, it is her friendship with Alice Cullen.

Alice is impatient to be her friend from the start of the story, and chides Edward, reminding him (she has psychic gifts) that she has seen a friendship between the two women as a potential future. While the rest of the younger Cullen family rage against the relationship, Alice anticipates what she and her new friend will do together.

For Bella the friendship is welcome. As she wrestles with her own awkwardness and seeming unawareness of her own beauty, she is slightly in awe of the 'exquisite elfin face' and willowy, graceful poise of Alice. Struggling as she does with her own fear of falling, she cannot help but notice Alice's fluid walk and almost dance-like movements, the smooth steps that would 'break any ballerina's heart'. She is amazed by Alice's voice and notes that when she laughs, 'the sound was all silver, like a wind chime.'

As their friendship grows, it is nurtured by Alice's presence with Bella at key points. Her father, Charlie Swan, is charmed by the exquisite vampire lady and extends greater trust to Bella when she is in the company of her new friend. It is Alice and Jasper who go to Phoenix with Bella when she flees from the attentions of the marauding tracker vampire James. As Bella recovers from her reckless cliff jump, it is Alice who reappears to renew the connection with the Cullen family. When the epic tale of Bella and the vampires reaches its most climactic moment in the potentially destructive confrontation with the Volturi, Alice appears, fresh from scouring the world to find another child like the half-human, half-vampire Renesmee.

Bella, like the Cullens, offers little resistance to Alice's exuberant, overstated extravagance. While Bella does not feel the need to imitate Alice's lifestyle choices, she seems to position herself as different, not critical.

It might seem that the debate at the heart of any critique of the *Twilight* series should centre round the epic romance of Edward and Bella or the tortured struggle that the Forks vampires have between their nature and their consciences. But to gloss over the character of Alice and her attitude towards money and possessions would be to miss a vital cultural signal.

The first comments to appear in the book about the use of resources might lead you to believe that the general tone is going to be one of concern for simple living and stewardship of the environment. Edward teases Bella about her gas-guzzling truck and informs her that 'the wasting of finite resources is everyone's business'. When she presses him about his diet of mountain lions, he responds: 'we have to be careful not to impact the environment with injudicious hunting. We try and focus on areas with an over-population of predators...' But after this promising start the tone changes. Let us consider how the family consumes other material possessions.

CLOTHES – CONFESSIONS OF A SHOPAHOLIC VAMPIRE

The Bella–Alice friendship does not have to be nurtured by constant agreement: in fact there is gentle friction between their personalities throughout the saga. Bella knows that 'her indifference to fashion is a constant thorn' in Alice's side. She quietly surrenders to Alice's outfitting for the wedding and stocking of the wardrobe in her new home.

Bella is not entirely passive. She is well aware of her 'boring jeans and T-shirt look' but reluctant to abandon it. She is helped by Edward's acute sense of smell to locate her familiar jeans and T-shirt amongst the welter of new clothes in the couple's cottage, so that she can journey up to the main house dressed in something familiar and comfortable.

But clothes run through the *Twilight* texts like a ribbon. The newly married Edward and Bella pull away from their wedding in a car that has a dozen pairs of designer shoes tied to the back. On arrival at their honeymoon destination, Bella discovers a suitcase full of new clothes and expensive French lingerie. When Bella emerges as a newly initiated vampire she notes that she is wearing silk and concludes that Alice must have dressed her.

Esme Cullen tells Jacob Black and his family that they have clothes to spare and often send brand-new clothes to the charity shop because 'Alice never really allows us to wear the same thing twice.'

CARS

Alice loves Porsches. Having stolen one during their race to save Edward from his attempt to have the Volturi kill him, she accepts his gift of a distinctive yellow model. Rosalie flaunts her wealth in a red convertible and the Cullen garage also contains a BMW M3 (note to non-petrolhead readers: this is a stylish sports saloon).

Edward gives his bride-to-be a Mercedes Guardian. To Bella it is just a car, albeit a powerful one, but after she parks it she discovers it being admired and is informed that the car is not generally available in Europe or America and is therefore likely to be a prized pre-release version. She remains vaguely aware of the conversation taking place about the car and notes that it has missile-proof glass and 4,000 pounds of body armour. This car is on loan, but even the ability to borrow it speaks of Edward's power and influence.

In the unpublished *Midnight Sun* Edward contemplates the possibility that the incandescent Rosalie might destroy a car belonging to the family but cannot allow himself to get too worried because, in his mind, 'It was just a toy'.

THE ACCESSORIES OF LIFE

The motto seems to be: *If you can have it, you should.* Alice decorates three miles of trees with shining lights. She provides 10,000 flowers for the festivities surrounding the wedding. She hangs priceless paintings on the walls of the cottage that she and the rest of the family create for Edward and Bella. When Bella stays with the Cullens she is installed in a designer bed made from wrought iron and decorated with sculpted metal roses. Notes from Alice arrive on ivory paper with petal-printed pages.

The nineteenth-century vampire heroes were predatory men or sexually voracious women. The contemporary vampires portrayed in the *Vampire Chronicles* of Anne Rice or the rag-tag misfits who coalesce around Buffy in *Buffy the Vampire Slayer* are glamorous outsiders, suspicious of the system and cynical about the realities of the non-vampire world. The popular vampire film, *The Lost Boys*, portrays a punk ethos and a raging, 'against the machine' nihilism.

You'll find none of that here. The relentless, conspicuous consumption that characterizes Alice throughout the entire epic is noted and celebrated by the storyline. No character emerges to question the ostentatious lifestyle that she presents. The Cullen children only downplay their wealth in the school context to avoid drawing too much attention to themselves.

Because Alice is clearly not identified as a negative character, her choices do not become polluted in the mind of the reader. The other characters are happy to accommodate those choices even if they don't feel compelled to participate in all of them.

This is vampire romance for the *Elle*, *Vogue* and *Cosmopolitan* reader, with Alice as the queen of the good times, dressing the rooms, dressing the Cullen characters, dressing the grounds and funding it all from stock-market success arising from her psychic gift.

While Carlisle Cullen works selflessly as a doctor, the real money engine is Alice. Her money is not earned. She hasn't started a wealth-creating scheme or enriched a local economy with new industry. She gets it by cheating the market. She gets it by magic.

But that's all right because she is a nice person, isn't it? She shares it. She's generous.

Some may argue that this exploration of a minor plot detail is over-zealous. Who cares how the money comes? But if we are to understand the writer's intent and the reader's reception of ideas in the books, then the assumptions underlying these details will help us. What values will *Twilight* reinforce or undermine? And how do they affect us?

Societies around the world may once have considered that they were making common cause in seeking a better life for all, by the way they voted, the conversations they had and the goods they consumed. With the rise of the consumer society we have forsaken that solidarity in favour of a quest for personal peace and prosperity. Wealth, fame and a media-orchestrated view of acceptable beauty appear to be the dominant notes in a consumer symphony that washes over us as we consume our mass-market fiction, our celebrity biographies, our advert-saturated surroundings, our brand-name clothing and the meticulous pursuit of the multi-orgasmic life.

The problem is not fashion, hairstyles, the admiration of certain types of physical beauty, the acquisition of excellent workmanship nor the desire for sexual pleasure. None of these choices or preferences is necessarily wrong. The problem arises when one's sense of worth and well-being is closely attuned to one's ability to possess the things that will signify that you are someone who 'belongs' and hence worthy of admiration. The *Twilight* series offers no consistent critique of this mindset at all. Instead, it celebrates it.

Bella is the only exception and is reluctant to have wealth lavished on her. But her resistance doesn't have an ideological edge and seems to be tied into not drawing attention to herself, partly because of her clumsiness and general introvert nature.

You cannot help but wonder why the Cullens had to be portrayed in this way. Indulge me for a moment as I pretend that Stephenie Meyer is having a small crisis in the character development exercises for the first *Twilight* book. A friend in the publishing industry agrees to critique her fledgling efforts which include an eco-friendly Cullen family who live in a carbon-neutral restored barn and make their own beautiful clothes using skills once common in society. Imagine the letter that the publisher friend sends:

Dear Steph,

Thanks for the sample chapter and the detailed overview of the plot and character development for the series. Love the erotic subtext and the melodramatic tensions of love in the midst of conflict.

Bit worried about the eco-friendly barn and all those plot points associated with organic wool and electric cars. It might help you sell a few books in Vermont and parts of southern California but it's not working for me.

Here's a reading list and some cultural

pointers that will help you capture the zeitgeist of this generation. Use this as your roadmap in the characterization process and I predict big things.

- *Watch MTV's* Cribs.
- *Watch America's Next Top Model.*
- *Buy a P Diddy album and Google him.*
- *Check out the Jennifer Lopez Video Collection.*
- *Get the Paris Hilton biography.*
- *Buy* The Hills *box set.*
- *Watch the* Gossip Girls *series.*
- *Have you ever watched* Extreme Makeover?
- *Google Trinny and Susannah.*

Make the whole thing more Charmed *than* Buffy the Vampire Slayer *and who knows how you might do. Keep Edward and Bella nice but get a bit of Romeo and Juliet or Wuthering Heights angst in there.*

> *Love you,*
> *Xavier*

Not likely, I know, but who would have thought that you could sell 70 million books about a vampire poster family for consumer capitalism to a generation that theoretically should be experiencing a wave of rebellion against the deep-vein acquisitiveness of their parents and wider society?

If we question the consumer values that Alice seems to symbolize, are we rejecting the idea of creativity and beauty and comfort? No. We believe all of those things are good in and of themselves. But we can explore them in simple ways that don't emphasize our differences, our wealth or our ownership of status symbols.

Readers of a cynical bent may be letting their minds wander through the netherlands of a cable TV schedule. There they see ministers sat on opulent thrones or pastors giving away cars. They compare the Armani suit of one preacher to the Hugo Boss of another. They contemplate the monogrammed gifts given to visiting preachers at high-profile crusades and the multiple homes, jets and marriages of some who come in the name of Jesus.

What right, then, does the church have to ask a nice, romantic-fiction-writing, Mormon lady whether she should have toned down Alice's cute capitalism?

Mainly because the Christian faith is running in the background of these novels. In Chapter 7, 'Is There Hope for My Soul?' we will examine how ideas to do with good and evil, God and creation, heaven and hell and the immortality of the soul intrude into the *Twilight* narrative again and again. The Christian God is given quite a bit of space in the spiritual backdrop to the story (alongside the spirit traditions of the Native American population and the idea of occult power that we can nurture and direct in the pursuit of our own ends).

Given that the Christian story is at least a reference point, what might this faith tradition have to say about the acquisitive culture that seems to characterize several members of the Cullen family?

In the Old Testament there is a book called the Song of Songs. The first seven chapters contain a lush description of erotic love. The poet's eye lingers on the form of his lover and notes that 'your cheeks are beautiful with ear-rings, your neck with strings of pearls.' He is consumed with her beauty, which he describes as without flaw. He describes her breasts as clusters of fruit. The Bible writers could not hold back from describing the beauty of what they saw and the feelings released within. Perfume and jewellery abound in their colourful descriptions.

The Bible, nevertheless, is full of seeming paradox, acknowledging and celebrating beauty, youth, vigour and wealth, but warning often of the snares that wealth brings and counselling justice in the midst of the acquisition of wealth.

This emerges through the prophetic tradition.

The Old Testament prophet Amos thunders: 'Hear this word, you cows of Bashan on Mount Samaria, you women who oppress the poor and crush the needy and say to your husbands, "Bring us some drinks!"' (Amos 4:1 NIV).

It resounds in the 'Jubilee' tradition in the book of Leviticus, which stipulated that land given in lieu of debt had to be returned after forty-nine years (Leviticus 25:28).

It is not a mere side-note in the biblical narrative. Calls to justice are found in over 1,000 verses (considerably more than those devoted to sexuality, incidentally). These verses contain critiques of economic systems, with Nehemiah reproaching his fellow countrymen for causing the newly arrived and previously exiled inhabitants of Jerusalem to swap slavery in a foreign land for slavery in the land of their birth. 'Give back to them immediately their fields, vineyards, olive groves and houses, and also the usury you are charging them – the hundredth part of the money, grain, new wine and oil' (Nehemiah 5:11 NIV). God tells the people bluntly not to bother coming to him with songs of worship if they are living unjust lives.

One of the most famous incidents in the ministry of Jesus concerns the unpopular interaction he had with the despised figure of the tax collector Zacchaeus, thought by the religious people of the day to be unclean and impure, and deeply unpopular with the ordinary people for exacting too much tax. Such collectors were deeply implicated in the tax system of the day, which is believed to have left 3 per cent of the population living in ease and 97 per cent as subsistence farmers. Ignoring such disapproval, Jesus showed Zacchaeus friendship and respect, even mercy. The fruit of Jesus' mercy was justice. Zacchaeus apologized and made restitution, thereby ensuring a more equitable distribution of money in Jericho.

Jesus chose to identify with the poor of his day, without despising the richer members of society. He spent time with Nicodemus and Joseph of Arimathea, both members of the ruling council of Jerusalem. But it is an unavoidable fact that he spent most of his time with the unfashionable Galileans and the marginal groups in society such as the shepherds, the tax collectors, the fishermen and the farmers.

He said of himself that he had nowhere to rest his head, and he commanded his disciples to go out in his name to preach and heal with the absolute minimum of material possessions (neither pack nor sandals), as they sought to share his love and compassion and the possibility that God's kingdom would come to earth (Luke 10:1–12).

He disappointed a rich young ruler when he commended to him the idea that he sell all that he had. He warned that it would be easier for a camel to go through a very narrow and low gate (the 'Eye of the Needle') in Jerusalem than it would be for a rich man to enter the kingdom of heaven.

These ideas were clearly deeply imprinted in the minds of his followers. Acts 2 records that the new believers had 'all things in common' and mutually supported one another. When this system broke down, deacons were appointed to ensure that the Greek widows were not neglected in the distribution of charity. James is emphatic in his denunciation of those who would keep the best seats in the church for the rich and powerful. Paul goads the Corinthians for slipping back into the socially stratified mealtime habits of Greek and Roman culture.

Jewish and Christian thought patterns converge to suggest attitudes towards money and property that allow for there to be periodic rebooting of the economy and a levelling of the playing-field of opportunity. This is enshrined in the law codes of the Hebrew Bible and demonstrably lived out by Jesus and his followers.

Take a moment to look around you. Your computer may have been produced using a process that, after long-term exposure, damages the lungs of the laboratory workers who produce the chips. Maybe the T-shirt that you're wearing was produced in a factory in China or South-east Asia where children work for fourteen hours per day to produce the brand names that our fictional Alice sends to a charity shop. The pension fund your family relies upon is invested in a stock-market system that must rely on 'usury and interest' and is manipulated on a daily basis by those who gamble on its movements.

The 10,000 flowers that adorn the Cullen mansion during the wedding of Edward and Bella may have come from a fairly traded, worker-friendly, organic farm if we were talking of real life and not fiction. But a huge amount of the cut flowers that we use in the West are flown from farms around the world where low-paid workers find their health quickly destroyed by the chemicals sprayed on the plants to prevent blight and encourage growth.

Justice in the world economy could consume chapters in this book and is the subject of many books anyway. I simply want to raise the questions. Some of the things that we enjoy in life, such as coffee, are fairly produced in many places, and we enjoy that luxury without contributing to injustice if we buy deliberately and exercise our consumer choice.

A series such as *Twilight* carries its assumptions deep into the heart of our culture. These books hold up some of the more endearing characters in this epic tale as living lives of unfettered luxury using money unfairly gained – and through occult power, moreover.

Lest there be any doubt about the commercial influence of these novels, a quick glance at the fan sites will confirm that *Twilight* is a franchise that is producing wealth far beyond the income stream from the books. Fashion ranges popularized by the characters are timed to come to market alongside the films. Mainstream brands in the retail world such as Nordstrom are part of this strategy. The *Twilight Saga* is deeply engaged in the world of mass-market consumerism.

Fans may protest that it is not the place of the romantic novelist to make value judgments about the settings in which their characters find themselves. But some of our most high-profile novelists clearly do offer a critique of the world around them. The multi-million-selling John Grisham uses the plotline of *The Runaway Jury* to ask questions of the tobacco industry. He examines the plight of the poor and homeless in *The*

Street Lawyer. Michael Crichton examines the dangers of nanotechnology in *The Prey*. Dan Brown questions the integrity of the New Testament and the church in *The Da Vinci Code*. It does seem eminently possible to write ideologically convincing fiction that appeals to the mass market.

What Stephenie Meyer has done here is not a 'sin of commission' where she has deliberately sought to promote the values of Consumer America. It's more likely a 'sin of omission', where she shares with many in her readership a disinclination to examine too deeply how everything is connected. You work hard, you get rich would seem to be the mantra. It is by no means that simple, and by featuring a group of rich young rulers at the heart of her story she has none too subtly endorsed one of the members of the unholy trinity of the unexamined life: money.

Which leads us to another member of that trinity – sex.

CHAPTER 5

SEX AND THE COUNTRY

Sex and the City and *Desperate Housewives* have brought erotically charged, notably urban storylines to mainstream television in recent years. The *Twilight Saga* introduces a somewhat gentler approach to the subject and sets developing passions in the rural context of Washington State.

The original target market for the books was teenagers. Given the point of view that dominates the narrative (Bella), a significant part of the interest in the series has always been her exploration of her own sexuality. For female readers with a growing awareness of their own desires, vulnerabilities and potential attractiveness, the journey of Bella from initial attraction to sexual conquest will be of great interest.

What emerges from the text is a curious mixture of social conservatism and sexual athleticism. It's very clear that promiscuity is not the norm for Bella or Edward and that they come to their relationship with very little sexual history.

Edward's choices have been a little limited, given the paucity of attractive vampires around the world who are also willing to give up drinking the blood of humans. In *Midnight Sun* he reflects on the sexual advances of the incredibly beautiful Tanya and reminds himself that her interest is 'not deep and hardly pure'.

Bella perceives herself as awkward and clumsy. As a result she is not socially confident and has not been sexually active. She quite emphatically informs her dad that she is a virgin, when he plucks up the courage to give her a fatherly lecture on sex before she is supposed to fly to Florida with Edward.

With a low expectation of her own impact on the opposite sex, Bella barely notices the stirrings among her male classmates following her arrival in Forks. Edward, with his mind-reading capacity, is alerted to Bella by the sordid imaginings of several of her admirers. Bella understands early in the story that she is beginning to attract Mike Newton and soon has interest from Tyler and Eric.

They hope that she might 'invite' them to the dance. She is completely phobic about dancing so hastily invents a trip to Seattle. This relieves her of the necessity of going to the dance but also allows her to let the boys down gently.

Were it not for the unpublished *Midnight Sun* we would only have a partial perspective on Edward's sexual awakening. As he learns to control his bloodlust, Edward discovers 'a new and strange desire'. New hungers were 'being shaken loose' by his increasing desire for her skin, her lips and her body. He is stirred by the 'soft cling of her blouse'. He barely knows how to cope and is concerned that this 'new kind of desire' will undermine his self-control, with disastrous consequences.

The other piece in the romantic jigsaw is Jacob Black. In an early flash of the greyer side of Bella's personality, we discover her flirting with Jacob, somewhat clumsily due to a lack of experience, in order to find out more information about the Cullens.

MORE THAN A FEELING?

Effective romantic fiction requires emotional depth to the characters. What is the basis for the affinity between Edward, Bella and Jacob?

EDWARD

Edward is wary of the actions and behaviour of those who see sex as a means of control and conquest. Bella discovers that Rosalie is ambivalent about her vampire status because her 'death' was not the result of disease or accident. She was raped by her husband-to-be and a number of other men and left for dead. Edward has to rescue Bella from a potential rape situation, with the *Midnight Sun* narrative filling out more detail than is available in the published books.

Edward is so angry with the sexual aggression that he discovers in the men's minds that he is on the verge of returning to his vigilante ways and killing them to protect others. Eventually he enlists the help of Carlisle, who captures them and deposits them many miles away. When the police arrest them, we discover that one of the men was a serial killer and rapist.

Edward is also a little taken aback at the explicit detail of the thought life of his fellow students once they begin to focus on Bella. As he rediscovers sexual desire his own thoughts begin to take a more erotic bent, spurred by his discovery of Bella as a compassionate human being. He steps away from a pornographic mindset that views women solely as objects, but he remains a man with commonplace male desires.

As they argue over the viability of their relationship, given that he is a vampire, Edward marvels at her and reflects that he believes that she could never hurt anyone. As he toys with the idea of whether she has a guardian angel, he tells himself that surely somebody that good would have one. He is in love with her character as well as being attracted to her body.

He reprimands himself for ever thinking that she was merely average-looking. He recalls the memory of her face in the minds that he read when she first came to the college and cannot help but think that it is obvious: she is beautiful as well as compassionate.

So Edward has fallen in love with all of Bella. His love is genuine, not simple lust. But how does Bella view the men in her life?

BELLA

In Chapter 3 we assessed Bella's nature. We noted that she examines life through the grid of beauty and the physical attributes of those she admires. Several of the beautiful women that she admires use their glamour like a weapon. Tanya simply desires to snare men for her pleasure. Rosalie does not want Edward but is seized with jealousy when he wants Bella.

Bella is clearly made of finer stuff than this, even if she does view life through a sensual filter. She reacts angrily when she feels that Jessica is framing her potential relationship with Edward simply around the idea that he's 'unbelievably gorgeous'. She is quick to respond, and works to find words to express what it is like when you discover the true Edward behind 'the face'.

Bella is drawn to Edward's willingness to take risks with his family and his future so that he can be with her. He is a suitable hero, having turned his back on the death and destruction of others, although we learn elsewhere in the story that Bella becomes so committed to Edward and Jacob that she will bury her own qualms about the possibility that they might both be killers.

JACOB AND BELLA

Bella knows that Jacob is attractive, but their relationship is more of a friendship than we initially see in the Bella–Edward relationship, which has to find its way out of conflict and then springs up through intense conversations. Bella and Jacob do things together. They mend bikes, they ride around the district. They have a relationship that is not based on having a *relationship*.

As her life unravels around her, Bella takes comfort in the fact that she believes that Jacob is a 'safe harbour'. She is attracted to Jacob and has been quite tactile with him. She is emotionally vulnerable following Edward's departure and her friendship with Jacob has lowered all her usual defences. As he wrestles with the changes in the tribe and himself, she embraces him, holding herself close to his chest. She tells him that he is 'sort of beautiful' – but is worried he might misconstrue the remark.

To be fair to Bella, she is honest about her boundaries with Jacob, but nevertheless tells him she can't 'imagine not liking being with you'. He is allowed to hold her hand. She is very conflicted. She doesn't want to give him false hope, but as she admits, she selfishly wants his company.

She wishes he could just be a friend, and is loath to risk another broken heart after the pain of losing Edward, but knows that she will let herself give him hope. She teeters on the brink of expressing physical affection more than once, despite feeling that her love for him is only a 'weak echo' of what she felt for the departed Edward.

The almost-romance twists and turns until the final chapters, where it becomes clear that Jacob's destiny will be with a grown-up Renesmee. There is an acceptance and comfort that is implicit between Jacob and Bella.

She does reject his physical advances, which include a borderline assault, but succumbs sometime later to an extended embrace and passionate kiss when he leaves to fight a battle from which he may never return. She is guilty, but Edward, having read Jacob's mind, blames him rather than her. Whatever is happening between Bella and Jacob, it is rooted in genuine friendship, not in lust. The relationship has a measure of depth and meaning.

As you would expect from a Mormon writer, who made it clear in several interviews that sex scenes with explicit descriptions would not be part of the *Twilight* project, the books frown on the promotion of sexual activity outside the boundaries of a genuine relationship.

But it would not be an exaggeration to suggest that one of the dominant threads for three-quarters of the whole *Twilight* narrative is concerned with the foreplay between Edward and Bella, as he seeks to avoid killing her in a frenzy of lovemaking, while she seeks to encourage him to take some risks and make love, nursing as she does the naïve belief that he will be able to control his desire for her blood and not break her with his superhuman strength.

THE CHRISTIAN VIEW OF SEX AND MARRIAGE

Many who would have moral scruples about promiscuity would nevertheless believe that a physical relationship between two people who genuinely like each other is permissible and does not have to happen within the boundaries of conventional marriage. This is the common position held by many – but it is still in tension with Christian sexual morality.

The Christian tradition, with respect to sex, has often been given a bad press. Within the life of the church over the last 2,000 years there have been groups who have introduced the idea that the body is to be despised and that sexuality is a necessary evil linked to procreation. This reached its height with a Victorian mentality, often sadly hypocritical, that deemed it impolite to talk about sexual matters. We are still living with this toxic legacy today.

All of this makes it hard for a Christian to ask genuine questions about sexual morality without being deemed repressed and joyless. Before asking some necessary questions about how Stephenie Meyer has written about sex in these books, perhaps we should state in brief and concise terms what a robust, healthy Christian view of sex and marriage might involve.

Sex is good

The Old Testament's Song of Songs, as we noted in Chapter 4, is frankly an erotic love poem. It's clearly a celebration of sexuality, with fulsome descriptions of both the character and the body of the Lover and the Beloved. The apostle Paul, writing to the Corinthians, does not discourage celibacy, believing as he does that this will help people focus on mission, but he also counsels his readers that if they are in a marriage relationship, they should be willing to be sexually active with each other and not deny their partner's pleasure. Old Testament law exempts men from military service in their emotionally charged and sexually active first year of marriage.

Sex has consequences

Although it is now technically possible to enjoy sex with a minimal risk of having children, the institution of marriage is still valuable, providing a stable environment for children to be nurtured. Children born outside wedlock, as study after study has shown, are far more likely to fail in education and life.

INTIMACY AND RESPONSIBILITIES

Asking people, in the marriage service, to make a covenant to each other before God and in front of witnesses is part of helping people to grasp that with intimacy comes responsibility. This responsibility relates to the emotional investment made by both parties in the act of lovemaking. Issues of trust, self-image, connection and emotional vulnerability are all wrapped up in the physical dance of love that good sex can be.

SEX CAN BE DESTRUCTIVE

Monogamy is healthy. Promiscuity isn't. Our society is having to inject teenage girls with a cancer vaccine to help reduce the escalating numbers of cervical cancer cases that we see as a result of high levels of sexual activity. How much of the inability to conceive that many women experience is related to the impact of sexually transmitted diseases and their enduring effect long after a person may have opted for a more settled lifestyle? Why is AIDS one of the largest killers in the world today?

MARRIAGE AND SOCIETY

Throughout the history of the world societies have developed customs, traditions or laws that provided help for widows, protected women in the aftermath of divorce and made clear what happened to property in the event of divorce or death. Until very recent times having an ill-defined relationship that had no legal foundation, let alone spiritual foundation, left women in a limbo when a relationship crumbled. Stable marriages are part of the bedrock of society – and a society that does not esteem them is following a self-destructive path.

The Christian tradition does not despise sex. It wants to celebrate it by giving it a context that protects it and nurtures it and can respond to all the different things that might happen as a result of sexual activity.

SEX IN *THE TWILIGHT SAGA*

Needless to say, there is barely a whiff of this in the pages of the epic we are studying. Edward's restraint is almost entirely based on pragmatism. He does not wish to harm the woman he loves. Bella, on the other hand, seems to subscribe to the school of thought which says that you should live in the moment and not over-analyse the future. She just wants him and is rarely the one who slows things down.

She reacts stormily to the idea of being married at nineteen. She believes that her mother, Renée, married too young and that was the reason that the relationship with Charlie foundered. She is deeply opposed to the idea of being the kind of girl who marries straight out of high school. The very fact that her mother gave her Victoria's Secret underwear when she was sixteen rather suggests that Renée not only felt that sexual activity was likely but that she wanted to ensure that her daughter arrived at the scene of passion nicely packaged.

The erotic passages in the book will linger in the imagination of the reader the longest. They are too numerous to spell out here but there are some patterns that might be helpful to highlight as we seek to understand the message that will remain.

AROUSAL

Whenever Edward touches Bella she becomes profoundly aroused. She talks of her bones turning soft and a hyperactivity of the heart (many times!). She has to remind herself to breathe and speaks of feeling dizzy (repeatedly). Her blood feels as if it is boiling and her breath comes in wild gasps. When she feels Edward may be relaxing his strict guidelines she crushes herself against him eagerly. Meyer returns the reader again and again to the almost orgasmic state that even the most minor sexual activity can provoke when the experience is first encountered. This state of unconsummated desire heightens the sexual tension for both our fictional couple and for the reader. Meyer avoids having to write sexually explicit scenes, which jar with her religious sensibilities and could cause controversy, given the target reader, by simply describing non-penetrative, clothes-on foreplay. The reader's imagination will do the rest.

SEDUCTION

Bella is frank about her own sexuality. Once she has fallen for Edward, she cheerfully admits that while, for some, love and lust might not keep the same company, for her they definitely do.

The logic is not spelt out but it would seem that she is confident that Edward's self-control, already demonstrated in his ability to kiss without thirsting after her blood, will suffice should the relationship become more physically expressive. She wants to undermine his sexual self-control because she believes he will be able to maintain his vampire self-control. She slowly pushes the boundaries, knowing that there is no excuse for her behaviour, but yearning for the thrill of intimacy nevertheless.

She presses him for birthday kisses and teases him as to whether he is tempted by her body. Everything becomes heightened when they are reunited after several months' separation. As he succumbs to an uncharacteristic moment of unguarded passion, she asks him whether he has changed his mind about the extent of their sexual relationship. He immediately regains control but she pouts: 'if we're not going to get carried away what's the point?'

Bella is very clear that she does not have the words to create a seduction scene – she tends to let her body do the talking. Once it has become clear that he will allow her to become a vampire, she wants to have sex with him while she is still human. Not knowing quite how to discuss this with him, she simply starts to undress him. When he resists she starts to undress herself. Edward, as always, eventually draws a boundary, but there is another partial undressing scenario before they eventually assert some self-control. Bella makes it clear again that she cannot see any reason to wait. She remains a virgin on a technicality related to the superpowers possessed by Edward.

The recklessness of desire that we see in Bella will not be an unknown emotion to readers. For some, however, the legitimization of these choices that is inferred by their attachment to the leading character in the story will reinforce the choices they make in real life. The reader is offered no reason to stay chaste, within the logic of the story.

CONSUMMATION

The final part of the series – *Breaking Dawn* – might be construed as being the most erotic section of the entire storyline. It starts with the newly married couple bathing nude together in the pool of their honeymoon home and then indulging in such active sex that they destroy all the pillows in the bedroom.

Edward hasn't quite mastered the control of his vampire strength yet, so Bella ends up badly bruised by his over-enthusiastic lovemaking. The newlyweds abstain from sex for a few days, before a middle-of-the-night incident, which only involves the shredding of expensive lingerie and a broken bed, allows Edward to practise being a little less energetic.

When Bella has given birth and become a vampire, the whole situation changes. Vampires don't sleep, so she and Edward use the nights to practise their new-found skills. It becomes clear that the other vampire couples enjoy similar extended bouts of lovemaking and

Bella cannot help but wonder how they are ever going to stop or slow down.

Our lovestruck couple have waited until they were married to enjoy (genital) sex. On the face of it, the message of the books might be construed as conservative and affirming of conventional morality. Their struggles to remain chaste and the overwhelming desire that takes them close to the boundaries that Edward has set will be familiar to many.

But the questions still remain. Does Bella have an underlying commitment to waiting until they are married? The answer would have to be no. Why does Edward hold back? Not particularly for reasons of morality but because of concerns for Bella's physical safety.

Will the clear descriptions of sexual arousal from Bella, repeated throughout the story, provoke sexual longing in the reader and legitimize or accelerate their own sexual activity? Do Bella's highly idealized descriptions of Edward's physicality create a 'wish dream' that for many readers is unobtainable? Slightly disappointingly, Stephenie Meyer follows entirely conventional romantic patterns here.

The underlying message of the *Twilight Saga* with respect to sex is: Go by your feelings, not by a wider, wiser value system.

So much for money and sex. What about power?

CHAPTER 6

THE OCCULT STING IN THE TALE

THREE DISTINCT SPIRITUALITIES weave their way through the *Twilight Saga*.

One strand explicitly draws upon traditional Christianity, with its visions of heaven, hell, creation and the afterlife. (We shall return to this in a later chapter.) Related to this Christian thread is the basic storyline about vampires, who were thought to be the spirits of the dead or demonic forces in some Christian traditions – though they play no part in the biblical narrative. Thirdly, shape-shifting mythologies associated with Native American spirituality also play their part.

Some readers will treat storylines relating to vampires and werewolves simply as fantasy. They will be engrossed in the story and will view the less rational aspects of the characters' lives just as a literary device.

But there is another thread that is constant throughout the saga and intensifies in the final book, *Breaking Dawn*. It is not a religious worldview that is easy to put a name to, and it does not tend to be expressed within conventional religious frameworks. It has to do with supernatural gifts.

The whole story revolves around the ability of Alice to foresee the future, Edward to read minds and Jasper to bring calm and feelings of peace by the exercise of a special gift. No religious explanation is given for the origins of these gifts. They are a 'given' within the story.

It becomes clear that others also have some form of gifting. In an undeveloped thread in *Midnight Sun*, Edward notes that Charlie Swan's thoughts are obscure to him, and not so accessible as those of the other mortals within the story, with the exception of Bella. The romance between Bella and Edward finds some of its emotional tension in the fact that he is unable to read her mind, a first for him and a source of both frustration and fascination.

Similar supernatural abilities are witnessed amongst the werewolves and the Volturi clan who police the vampire world. The werewolves are able to communicate via an ethereal 'group mind'.

Several of the Volturi have spiritual power that can affect matter and change the circumstances of a situation. The leading Volturi, Aro, is able to hear every thought you ever had, simply by touching you. Another Volturi leader, Marcus, can discern relationships and their intensity. A bodyguard, Jane, can cause intense pain with a single thought. One of the former bodyguards, Eleazar, becomes helpful to the Cullen family. His gift is to know what special powers any vampire might have.

Another guard, Chelsea, can influence the emotional ties between people. She can also encourage greater cooperation. Alec, another bodyguard, is able to send a creeping mist, which incapacitates those it touches.

The allies of the Cullens have their own gifts. Kate can create electric power which can injure anyone it touches. Zafrina can strike you blind. Benjamin can influence the elements, breaking up the ground and causing chasms to appear.

Perhaps the most striking power is that which is eventually manifested through Bella. She is able to thwart the power of others by creating a shield of protection around herself, and in time others. Jane and Alec cannot hurt her and Demetri, who senses where people are, cannot find her.

While the gifts attributed to various characters may seem fantastic, the belief in such gifts is quite widespread, to the point where we have words for them, and group them under the term 'extra-sensory perception' (ESP). The gift that Alice has is called *clairvoyance*. The werewolves have a *clairaudience* ability. The ability of Aro is close to a gift known as *clairsentience*. The insights attributed to Eleazar are known as *claircognizance*.

There are several schools of thought about how human beings come to acquire these abilities, the existence of which is supported by widespread anecdote but has proved hard to pin down in laboratory conditions. The *Twilight Saga* offers its own clues. Carlisle has told Edward that his theory is that the vampires have brought their strongest human traits into their new-life and that their vampire power intensifies that gifting.

Eleazar talks of the 'latent' ability of humans to use these gifts, describing them as 'nebulous'. As he gets to know Bella he is amazed at her ability to 'shield' herself against the psychic abilities of others. Since she had this gift before becoming a vampire, it is noted as 'a rather powerful latent talent'.

The use of the word *latent* here is important, because this is quite a widespread belief. As an example, some occult and religious groups around the world subscribe to the idea that the city of Atlantis, a mythical land thought to have sunk beneath the Atlantic during a worldwide cataclysm, was at the heart of a culture where the abilities of Edward and Alice would have been commonplace.

The New Age writer Dr Shirley McCune, one of the authors of *The Light Shall Set You Free*, notes the core beliefs surrounding the myth:

> *All humans have the natural ability to perceive dimensions higher than the Third... In Atlantis, humans in embodiment accepted this mode of operation and perception as normal behavior. The Atlanteans operated on this superior level of existence, connected to their Higher Selves. With the fall of Atlantis, humanity experienced a struggle for survival and became aware of the lower self, dominated by the will of the ego. Now after thousands of years of evolution, most people have forgotten... how to connect with higher dimensions...*

The Atlantean myth arose out of the writings of Plato and was reinforced in the popular imagination by the retelling of the story by Sir Francis Bacon, the man whose utopian vision shaped the mindset of those who established the United States of America. Bacon (1561–1626), an Elizabethan scientist and philosopher, was also a mystic whose book *The New Atlantis* was highly influential.

Mainstream Christianity also recognizes the possibilities of gifts similar to those portrayed in the *Twilight* story. Jesus is able to know the thoughts of those around him and sometimes responds before criticism is uttered verbally:

> *When the Pharisee who had invited him saw this, he said to himself, 'If this man were a prophet, he would know who is touching him and what kind of woman she is — that she is a sinner.'*
>
> *Jesus answered him, 'Simon, I have something to tell you.'*
>
> *'Tell me, teacher', he said.*
>
> LUKE 7:39–40 NIV

The epistles of Paul outline similar gifts at work within the early church:

> *There are different kinds of gifts, but the same Spirit. There are different kinds of service, but the same Lord. There are different kinds of working,*

but the same God works all of them in all men.

Now to each one the manifestation of the Spirit is given for the common good. To one there is given through the Spirit the message of wisdom, to another the message of knowledge by means of the same Spirit, to another faith by the same Spirit, to another gifts of healing by that one Spirit, to another miraculous powers, to another prophecy, to another distinguishing between spirits, to another speaking in different kinds of tongues, and to still another the interpretation of tongues. All these are the work of one and the same Spirit, and he gives them to each one, just as he determines.

1 Corinthians 12:4–11 niv

Some Christians believe that these supernatural gifts were only exercised by the generation of disciples who had been with Jesus and that they no longer operate today. A small minority of people believe that everyone in humanity was gifted in this way from the dawn of creation but that man's sin and rebellion against God led to a loss of these abilities. In this view, they can be acquired again by cooperating with God through the work of the Holy Spirit. The apparent exercise of these gifts by others who are not working within the boundaries of conventional Christianity is seen, according to this viewpoint, as a work of the devil, if indeed it can be proved to be genuine.

A much more widely accepted view within Christian theology is that all such genuine gifts are from God. The word *charism*, used in the original Greek in 1 Corinthians 12, means 'a gift of grace'.

Any such gifts are therefore perceived as the work of God, and to be given by the Holy Spirit in the way and to whom God chooses. This lies in stark contrast to the idea that these gifts are latent – that they can be reawakened, trained as a reflex and used at the whim of the mind of man.

Storylines about our power to control the elements or the lives of others are at the heart of much popular literature. When we discover such stories in the context of the *Harry Potter* series, where they are surrounded by ideas to do with ritual, incantation and the other trappings of symbolic magic, it will be easy for us to hold them at arm's length and dismiss their import, as they are merely myths and fables.

The *Twilight* treatment is rather different. *Breaking Dawn* specifically suggests that these gifts are available to *non*-vampires, even if they use them rather weakly. Note that there is no suggestion at any point in the narrative that it is necessary to say special words or undertake special rituals in order to use this power. The storyline suggests that to use the mind in this way is a latent ability that can be trained.

Bella wants to play a part in the defence of herself, her newborn child and the wider Cullen family. Edward is loath to be the one who trains her, as he finds it impossible to think of her as a target. The sympathetic vampire Kate is therefore the one who begins to help her, not merely to use her new strength but also to summon up her wider psychic abilities. When she becomes worried about a threat to her child, she discovers that her rage increases the range of her protective shield.

She extends her ability as she seeks to protect group members from the blindness that Zafrina temporarily inflicts upon them. The stage is now set for the climactic battle between the Cullens and the Volturi. A decisive factor in the decision of the Volturi to retreat strategically, having debated the legitimacy of Renesmee, is their knowledge that the shield that Bella has thrown around those sympathetic to her cause is impenetrable by all the normal methods that the Volturi use to subjugate their enemies.

These ideas about the latent gifts of the mind surface in the bestselling sequel to *The Da Vinci Code*,

Dan Brown's *The Lost Symbol*. The core idea behind this new bestseller is this: The religious traditions of the world, if properly understood, suggest that as humans we too are gods. Brown suggests through his plotline that Freemasonry and Rosicrucianism have perhaps best understood this and have made great strides in encouraging people to think in this way.

He weaves in esoteric thought from the writings of Isaac Newton and Sir Francis Bacon, two renowned scientific figures who sought to combine the disciplines of scientific research and mystical speculation. He also includes comment and speculation surrounding the ideas of quantum physics to further bolster the idea that what we regard as the supernatural is in fact a natural ability that can be exercised by the training of the mind and through acts of will.

If we therefore bear in mind that the influence of The *Twilight Saga* and *The Lost Symbol* is likely to extend to at least 100 million readers, we would not be stretching a point if we were to say that perhaps one in twenty of the people in nations where there is widespread literacy are reading material that will subtly (and in the case of Dan Brown, directly) suggest that the supernatural acts of Jesus are not marks of his relationship with the divine, but simply the skills of a trained mind. Jesus, in this view, then simply becomes a teacher whose ethics are highly regarded.

Both books present a world in which legitimate personal spiritual power is available outside the context of a relationship with God and the empowerment of the Holy Spirit. *The Lost Symbol* further suggests that perfectly rational and well-respected men and women are increasingly the champions of ideas surrounding the possibility of natural power, personally exercised.

Research into the paranormal is a polarizing activity. Those who claim supernatural gifts, discovered and exercised without connection to religious affiliation, claim that their best practitioners' skill can be verified by experiment. What if they are right?

Some Christians would follow the lead of the late Professor Donald Mackay, who observed:

> *It is impossible for a scientific discovery given by God to contradict a Word given by God. If therefore a scientific discovery, as distinct from scientific speculation, contradicts what we have believed by the Bible, it is not a question of error in God's Word, but of error in our way of interpreting it. Far from 'defending' the Bible against scientific discovery, the Christian has a duty to welcome thankfully, as from the same*

Giver, whatever light each may throw upon the other. This is the 'freedom' of a fully Christian devotion to the God of Truth.

> D. M. MACKAY, 'SCIENCE AND THE BIBLE' IN *THE OPEN MIND AND OTHER ESSAYS* (ED. MELVIN TINKER, IVP, 1988, P. 150)

As we have already noted, Paul in 1 Corinthians 12 states that these gifts are from God. The Bible infers that when they are exercised by those who are not followers of Christ, they are the work of a third class of being, neither human nor God. Known as either demons or angels, depending on whether they are in league with God or against him, these spiritual creatures can inspire supernatural knowledge in humans. An incident in the Book of Acts illustrates this:

Once when we were going to the place of prayer, we were met by a slave girl who had a spirit by which she predicted the future. She earned a great deal of money for her owners by fortune-telling. This girl followed Paul and the rest of us, shouting, 'These men are servants of the Most High God, who are telling you the way to be saved.' She kept this up for many days. Finally Paul became so troubled that he turned around and said to the spirit, 'In the name of

Jesus Christ I command you to come out of her!'
At that moment the spirit left her.

When the owners of the slave girl realized
that their hope of making money was gone, they
seized Paul and Silas and dragged them into the
market-place to face the authorities.

ACTS 16:16–19 NIV

Whatever success science has in verifying the abilities described in the *Twilight Saga*, the Bible offers an explanation that lies outside the realms of the mind-powered, little-gods view inherent in the work of Dan Brown and Stephenie Meyer.

The other idea that is latent in both books is that the knowledge of these things has to be deposited with an elite group. In the *Twilight Saga* the superhuman vampires and werewolves possess this power in abundance. In *The Lost Symbol* it is the powerful and secretive Freemasons who have it. In both books the propensity for evil even amongst the elite groups who hold the secrets infers that they are definitely too dangerous for the ordinary man and woman. This should always ring a warning bell. When our cultural narratives tell us to trust an elite (such as bankers, for example), we are in danger of losing our critical sharpness. Jesus recruited his followers from outside the elite (shepherds, fishermen and political zealots) and constantly critiqued the elites of his day (Pharisees, Sadducees and scribes). Should we trust books that infer that we should defer to the 'powerful and the wise'? Maybe not.

There is, of course, an undeniable glamour about the mystical, the secret and the powerful, especially if we do not have strong institutions that will speak on our behalf to those in positions of strength. If we are wary of a society which has become atomized and lost its neighbourhood and community bonds, then how cautious should we be of those who promote an elitist view of spiritual knowledge, rather than an open, community-based celebration of the goodness of God, expressed in Jesus?

When those unique gifts are constantly linked to those who are beautiful, accomplished, intellectual and financially powerful, we should perhaps ask ourselves whether these are the heroes that we really desire, despite our initial admiration.

The book of Isaiah spoke of a suffering servant who would come to visit the people of Israel. The suffering servant never loomed quite so large in the political imagination of Jesus' day as the warrior king that many sought in order to drive out the Romans.

He had no beauty or majesty to attract us to him, nothing in his appearance that we should desire him. He was despised and rejected by men, a man of sorrows, and familiar with suffering. Like one from whom men hide their faces he was despised, and we esteemed him not.

ISAIAH 53:2–3 NIV

Jesus had amazed the people with his miracle power. Following the feeding of the 5,000, they sought to take him to Jerusalem to make him a King and so initiate a popular uprising. However, he refused to be the warrior king and would later die on the cross, days after he had washed the feet of his disciples as an illustration of how they should serve one another. The servant king suffered a painful death – only to triumph over all the forces that conspired against him by rising from the dead and empowering his disciples to continue his work of love, grace, mercy and spiritual restoration.

If spiritual power is a gift of God, it comes with boundaries and inside the framework of the accountability that the life of Jesus suggests to us. If the fiction of Dan Brown or Stephenie Meyer does have any basis in reality, have they warned us of the habitually evil but given us little guidance beyond 'don't kill people'? In the absence of the absolute God, do we make up our own morality? How are good and evil reflected in the *Twilight Saga*?

It is to this we now turn as we seek to understand how the *Twilight* epic treats the ideas at the heart of conventional Christianity.

CHAPTER 7

IS THERE HOPE FOR MY

SOUL?

WHILE MUCH OF the *Twilight* story is told from the perspective of Bella, the moral centre of the story is found in the interplay between the beliefs of Edward and Carlisle. These are rooted in the familiar Judaeo-Christian narrative about God, creation, moral choice and our eternal destiny, either in heaven or in hell.

We will return to these in due course, but first let's take Bella's religious temperature. Like many, Bella can adopt the language of religion despite having little or no church involvement. She professes to be 'devoid of belief' and tells Edward that she won't need heaven if she can be with him. But she also describes Jacob as a 'gift from the gods', as well as sarcastically deriding his new-found desire to be with Sam Uley and his fellow werewolves with the putdown, 'Now you've seen the light, hallelujah' – a comment derived from a popular religious metaphor. She can't conceive of a deity but it's clear that if there is one, he has to be ready to accept Carlisle Cullen, whom she regards as something close to a saint.

We're reading a fictional story with fantastical elements. No one expects the exactness of a theological creed. What is noticeably absent from the story, however, is any significant mention of Jesus or the Holy Spirit – which, given the spiritual undertones of the books, would not be implausible: holy and faithful men and women appear in many a modern fantasy, for instance in Jim Butcher's Harry Dresden stories, which feature plenty of vampires. There is no need for the Holy Spirit in the spiritual world of the werewolves and vampires in the *Twilight* stories, because much of what the Spirit does within the Christian tradition is now promoted as a mind skill, a latent talent to be cultivated and used at will.

Jesus only figures in the most marginal way in the discussions of religion that take place within the book. Bella expresses surprise that the Cullens have a large wooden cross in the house. It reflects Carlisle's respect for his own spiritual roots prior to becoming a vampire. Edward assures her that the idea that it's effective in driving out vampires is simply superstition.

The books explore ideas of forgiveness, moral restraint and the personal goodness of several characters, while ignoring any idea that Jesus' life, death and resurrection might have a bearing on our relationship with God. But God is nevertheless a constant in the thought patterns of both Carlisle and Edward. The God that we see in the *Twilight Saga* feels like the God of the Deists, who created the world, gave us moral frameworks and now leaves us largely in peace to work out how we might live until he intervenes in history again.

Some of the dialogue hints at godlike qualities among the vampires. The Romanian vampires who were displaced by the Volturi talk of having spent centuries 'contemplating their divinity' before realizing their fallibility. The Volturi leader Aro, speaking with poetic licence, one assumes, wonders if there's been anybody among gods and mortals who has seen things quite so clearly as he and Edward.

Ideas and word pictures that have their origins in the Bible are common throughout the text. Is this because Stephenie Meyer simply puts them into the characters' mouths because she is familiar with such language, or, more generously, because she wants to create a disturbing echo of religion and a pleasing complexity in the novels' tone? Or should we just assume that characters in an American setting would be familiar with the meaning of these phrases, because so many people in the USA have contact with church at some point in their life?

Religious references certainly abound within the text. Edward murmurs to Bella that the 'lion has fallen in love with the lamb', which has something of a biblical ring about it, although the more common metaphor of animal kingdom togetherness is found in Isaiah 11:6, which talks of an ideal time when the wolves will exist peacefully with the lambs!

Edward also evokes the imagery of the prodigal son (a parable from the teaching of Jesus) to describe the welcome he receives on his return from his self-imposed exile. He can't push a metaphor too far, of course, because the original prodigal took half the father's fortune and returned in disgrace. Edward merely left for a while.

Jacob shows a familiarity with spiritual concepts outside Native American spirituality when he reflects that Bella has a martyr-like quality that would have seen her volunteering to go to the lions during the persecutions suffered by the early church. Comparisons are also drawn between the flood myths of the Quiluete Indians and the story of Noah, with the Indians surviving by tying their canoes to the top of tall trees.

Jacob also quotes the biblical King Solomon's predicament – where he has to try to establish who is the real mother of a baby – to help explain how the tension between Edward, Jacob and Bella over her conflicting emotions and love for both of them, can be ended. Bella, despite her professed lack of belief, is familiar with the story.

Organized religion barely intrudes, however. Edward and Bella are married by the local Lutheran minister. His daughter Angela is a significant, albeit minor, figure in the overall plot. Edward is convinced of her goodness and actually seeks to avoid reading her mind too much, to give her some privacy. She shows unconditional and undemanding love towards Bella and is supportive without being intrusive. Edward describes her as follows in *Midnight Sun*:

> *She was oddly content for a teenager. Happy. Perhaps this was the reason for her unusual kindness – she was one of those rare people who had what they wanted and wanted what they had. If she wasn't paying attention to her teachers and her notes, she was thinking of the twin little brothers she was taking to the beach this weekend – anticipating their excitement with*

an almost maternal pleasure. She cared for them often, but was not resentful of this fact.

Other than Carlisle Cullen, Angela is one of the few characters in the books who receives an unambiguous endorsement.

Before we plunge into ideas relating to heaven and hell and right and wrong, perhaps we should pause and clarify our theological ideas about vampires, because it has a bearing on our understanding of Edward's predicament with respect to his soul.

VAMPIRE 'THEOLOGY'

Vampire myths are common in cultures around the world. When those myths came in contact with conventional Christianity, the blame for vampire-like activities began to fall on demons, whose existence was already acknowledged within the biblical literature. The absence in the Bible of any story with vampire overtones, and the lack of any concrete evidence, have not prevented plenty of spiritual speculation.

Such speculation was a cottage industry in the centuries up until the Protestant Reformation, with spiritual power being attributed to a panoply of saints, relics and places. Within that largely religious environment there was a great deal of discussion about when, exactly, the soul left the body at the point of death. Fertile imaginations began to suggest that maybe alleged vampire activity was the work of restless spirits who had not yet found their resting-place after death. As the mythology grew the idea was gradually accepted that one vampire might 'initiate' another, as we saw in Chapter 2.

We are not going to criticize Stephenie Meyer for using vampires as a literary device. But we do need to be really clear about the biblical understanding of life after death.

It would seem that prior to the coming of Christ, all of those who awaited their destiny in a life after death were believed to have gone to Hades, or Sheol. Sheol was regarded with some apprehension by some of the Old Testament writers, but the book of Job describes it in more positive terms as a place of waiting:

There the wicked cease from troubling, and there the weary are at rest. There the prisoners are at ease together, they hear not the voice of the taskmaster. The small and great are there, and the slave is free from his master.

Job 3:17–19 (RSV)

There was an expectation of an ultimate resurrection:

Thy dead shall live, the bodies shall rise. O dwellers in the dust, awake and sing for joy!

ISAIAH 26:19 (RSV)

The Christian theologian Peter Cotterell, writing in *I Want to Know What the Bible Says About Death* (Kingsway Publications, 1979) says this of the time in between death and judgment:

But once we leave this universe, time no longer exists... We tend unthinkingly to transfer our patterns of thought and speech, suited to this world, over to the next world, where they are quite out of place... categories of before and after simply don't apply to the next life.

Christ made it clear in his words on the cross that the repentant thief would join him that night in Paradise (Luke 23:39–43). A new day had dawned. For those who entered into a relationship with God through Jesus, Paradise awaited after death. For the rest, Sheol was their resting-place until the day of judgment.

Other scriptures affirm the idea that we die once, and then comes a final judgment (Hebrews 9:27). Paul, writing to the Corinthians, tells us that at death we become absent from the body and present with the Lord (2 Corinthians 5:8).

Incidents in the life of Jesus hint that God can allow the recall of some, albeit for a limited time and a specific purpose. This is particularly true of the event at the Mount of Transfiguration, where the three disciples attending Jesus see with awe that the Old Testament figures of Elijah and Moses are standing beside him and conversing with him.

The Bible gives sustenance to the idea that there may be spiritual realities beyond our temporal existence, but it lends no support to the idea that bloodsucking zombies or well-dressed vampires can walk the earth, let alone discuss the finer points of whether a vampire has a soul and whether they will find acceptance before God and enter heaven.

But at the heart of the *Twilight Saga* is a man of peace, whose character seems to have been shaped by an involvement with Christianity before his unfortunate initiation as a vampire. What undercurrents inform the life of Carlisle Cullen?

THE MAN OF PEACE

Carlisle is the son of a sixteenth-century Anglican clergyman who is active in persecuting dissident groups within the society of his day. One of his key roles over and beyond finding witches and heretics is the hunting down of vampires. Carlisle is beginning to doubt some of the certainties that his father holds to and is distressed by the fact that innocent people are dying as a result. The troubled Carlisle is, however, successful in tracking down genuine vampires and takes comfort in the fact that he is helping to protect people from a great evil.

During one such hunt he is fatally attacked by vampires, is himself transformed, and must hide himself away lest he too be hunted down and killed. For many lonely years he struggles alone, but having trained himself not to lust for human blood and only to feed on animals, he eventually finds some contentment as a doctor. He has moved away from the vampire clans around the world and slowly creates a family around himself by turning people on the verge of death into vampires, whom he in turn can train to drink only from animals.

He clings obstinately to the faith of his pre-vampire days and tells Bella: 'But never, in the nearly 400 years now since I was born, have I ever seen anything to make me doubt whether God exists in some form or another.'

He's not unaware that in the great scheme of things, vampires do not qualify as candidates for the heaven of the Judaeo-Christian God. 'By all accounts, we were damned regardless. But I hope, maybe foolishly, that we'll get some measure of credit for trying.' This is not the way things work in the New Testament: 'For it is by grace you have been saved, through faith … not by works, so that no-one can boast.' (Ephesians 2:8–9). But remembering that this is a story, let's give Carlisle the benefit of the doubt.

Having decided that he will not take human life or drink human blood, Carlisle follows his compelling logic and becomes a peacemaker and a restorer of life. He is not portrayed as a complete pacifist and is willing to defend his friends against predatory vampires, but where he does so, it would be fair to say that he has embraced a 'just war' philosophy with very clear boundaries.

His intent is made clear by his active pursuit of peace. Upon settling in the area around Forks, he approaches Ephraim Black, the local Indian leader, with a proposal for peace between the warring wolves and vampires. The vampires stay away from the area around the reservation and make a commitment not to hunt humans, nor to initiate new vampires in that area of Washington State.

Carlisle continues to press home the logic of his stance throughout the story. He has rarely relaxed his unwavering commitment throughout 400 years, only allowing Rosalie to exact revenge on her human killers, the men who had raped her and left her to die.

In *Midnight Sun* he states his position very clearly when faced with a militant Rosalie, who is intent on killing Bella to prevent the vampires from being revealed to the local community:

> *Carlisle never compromised.*
>
> *'I know you mean well, Rosalie, but… I'd like very much for our family to be worth protecting. The occasional… accident or lapse in control is a regrettable part of who we are.' It was very like him to include himself in the plural, though he had never had such a lapse himself. 'To murder a blameless child in cold blood is another thing entirely. I believe the risk she presents, whether she speaks her suspicions or not, is nothing to the greater risk. If we make exceptions to protect ourselves, we risk something much more important. We risk losing the essence of who we are.'*
>
> *Rosalie scowled. 'It's just being responsible.'*

*'It's being callous', Carlisle corrected
gently. 'Every life is precious.'*

His abhorrence of violence is deep-seated. While he is
prepared to use it against the vampire horde that arrive
with the Volturi, Edward notes that even as Carlisle
gives Jasper permission to train the others for battle,
there is pain in his eyes. 'No one hated violence more
than Carlisle.'

He is also a man of his word and will not renege
on his treaty with the wolves when a potential ally seeks
to trade allegiance in the forthcoming conflict, with the
opportunity for revenge against the wolves, who had
killed the vampire Laurent when he had threatened to
attack Bella. Carlisle and Edward restrain the Denali
vampires after Caius kills Irena in an attempt to ignite
violence between the Volturi and those who were siding
with the Cullens.

Aro, the Volturi chieftain, has marvelled in the
past at Carlisle's steadfast commitment and remarks
that he 'has no sense of [his] own self-interest'.

This commitment to dignity, tolerance and
forgiveness becomes part of the ethical commitment of
those around Carlisle. Edward asks him to deal with the
man who led the attack on Bella in Port Angeles. (The
very request suggests the warmth and trust of a secure

family where a father's advice is welcomed and sought.) Edward looks to him as a moral compass and expresses his own wariness of war and violence in his comment to Bella about 'the idealised glory of war' that surrounded young men of his age in the years before the 1918 great flu epidemic, which brought Edward close to death and resulted in his initiation as a vampire by Carlisle.

Several other characters seem to have an instinct towards tolerance and peace-making. The young wolf, Seth, constantly defuses potential conflict. Alice never shared the reservations of the other Cullens about Bella. Bella simply can't see why there should be any conflict between the wolves and the vampires and declares herself to be like the neutral nation of Switzerland when it comes to these centuries-old rivalries.

It only takes one voice sometimes to cause many to stop and reflect on their previously instinctive choices. Carlisle is that one voice among the bloodthirsty vampires. Following his example, Edward, Bella and Renesmee speak through their lives to Nuhuel, who realizes that the super-race ambitions of his vampire father are not the only way forward for him, and that he can find support for his latent desire for peace.

Carlisle's influence on his adopted family also points us to another undercurrent that eddies throughout the five books. Who is helping our key characters find their way in the world? Bella experiences the unconditional love of Charlie Swan and, as best he can, he seeks to help her find good boundaries. It's clear that her mother, Renée, loves her, but in a curious role reversal, it is often Bella who has the maturity of 'a thirty-five year old'. Edward, clearly influenced by the positive model of marriage that he sees in Carlisle and Esme, wants to make a covenant commitment to Bella in a ceremony of marriage. Bella, somewhat prejudiced by the failure of her parents' marriage, does not value the idea as highly as he does.

But Bella instinctively knows the value of the family. As Caius seeks an excuse to attack the Cullens during the climactic confrontation over Renesmee, Bella reflects that maybe he doesn't understand real families who are 'in relationships based on love rather than just the love of power'.

Garrett, a vampire who chooses to support the Cullens, makes an impassioned speech to the Volturi and the gathered vampire 'witnesses':

> *I have witnessed the bonds within this family...*
> *it seems to me that intrinsic to this intense family*
> *binding – that which makes them possible at all*
> *– is the peaceful character of this life of sacrifice.*

There is no aggression here... there is no thought for domination.

If there is an element in the stories where the *Twilight Saga* comes close to expressing an authentic '*Twilight* gospel', then this is it. The commitment of Carlisle to being a 'god-fearing' man, despite his unpromising vampire status, echoes through his life and into the lives of others as he embraces selflessness, sacrifice and self-control. He resists violence and has no thought for domination.

If Carlisle's faith journey has led him to be a man of peace, where is Edward's journey leading him?

CHAPTER 8

TWILIGHT OF THE SOUL

IF THERE'S ONE CHARACTER in the *Twilight* drama who really thinks about life and destiny in a way that is visible to the reader, it is Edward. He vacillates between a fairly conventional, God-orientated view of morality and life and more pagan ideas about the role of fate. He uses the imagery of religion in mapping out his emotions and responses rather than as a precise guide to his thinking on spirituality.

Like his adoptive mother Esme, he talks of the 'fates', mythical creatures who (according to Greek and Roman mythology) are supposed to attach themselves to humans three days after birth and guide you to your destiny. He is concerned that Bella's 'fate' is a bitter harpy with no concern for her well-being. He would rather believe that she has a guardian angel but can only conclude that, given her accident-prone nature, she has instead a reckless angel.

Bella prefers to believe that Edward might be an Archangel, given the beauty of his voice. He in turn speculates whether she is a demon sent to taunt him and inflame both his human and his vampire desires.

His thoughts about God, sin and forgiveness emerge within the first paragraphs of the unpublished *Midnight Sun*. School, he reflects, is like Purgatory, a halfway house between earth and heaven, where some Catholics believe that sins omitted during times of confession and repentance on earth can be forgiven if the right prayers are said by the right people. If it *was* possible to atone for his sins, he reasons, surely his attendance at school would count in some way.

Unlike Carlisle, Edward believes that there is no way back for him. Not only is he a vampire, but he has been unable to show the restraint that Carlisle has demonstrated for the last 400 years. During a period of rebellion he returned to hunting humans, but limited himself to bad and dangerous men. Edward feels that the god-like vigilante violence that he exacted on killers and murderers cannot be forgiven. He tells Bella that there must be boundaries in life and that he has frequently disobeyed God's injunction not to murder.

Others are not so convinced. Emmett chastises him and warns that eternity is a long time to wallow in guilt. Carlisle says this of Edward: 'His strength, his goodness, the brightness that shines out of him – and it only fuels that hope, that faith more than ever. How could there not be more for one such as Edward?'

It is hard to speculate about what a theology of grace might look like for a vampire. Edward's feelings about his soul might be consistent with the inner logic of vampire mythology, but they can't be dislodged by messages of grace from Carlisle – not least because the whole plot structure and the romantic and sexual tension between Edward and Bella depends on Edward showing restraint, because of his fear of hurting her and because he is unwilling to make her a vampire out of concern for her soul.

Stephenie Meyer even has Edward wade into the middle of the creation–evolution debate. He doesn't dismiss evolution, but comments that he finds it hard to believe that life on Earth just happened on its own. Maybe God created vampires, he muses to Bella during one of their getting-to-know-you dates. Having opened a scientific and theological can of worms, Meyer swiftly moves on and the character of Edward sticks to speculating on the soul thereafter.

Edward is adamant that there is no afterlife for the vampire and is convinced that Bella will hate him for stealing her soul, should he offer her a vampire new birth. Bella, despite her ambivalence about spiritual matters, eventually makes it clear to him that she will play by his rules, as she doesn't want to take any chances with his soul and its eternal destiny.

Edward returns to the concern about her soul throughout the plot. He is unwilling to condemn her to 'an eternity of night'. His reluctance to make her a vampire causes him to leave Forks altogether so that she can move on in her life and discover love with a human. Even after his return he cannot believe that she is eager for what he perceives to be her eternal damnation, and remains adamant that he will not destroy her soul. She in turn believes his experience of near-death at the hands of the Volturi almost caused him to believe that maybe Carlisle was right and that he does hold out some hope for a life in eternity.

Edward is convinced that should the day come when someone is victorious in conflict and destroys him with fire, he will go to hell, existing in the seventh circle, the fictional abode of those guilty of violence against God, humanity and animals (according to medieval cosmology, as set out in Dante's *Inferno* – the first circle being for minor sinners, the ninth and last being for the very worst). He flippantly suggests that he allowed himself to drift into a relationship with Bella that had no real chance of success because, if he was going to hell anyway, he might as well enjoy it.

Eventually he succumbs to his desire for Bella and seems ready to exchange fear about the future for happiness in the here and now. He consents to making her a vampire.

There is much to admire about Edward. He loves goodness and responds to it when he witnesses it in the lives of Esme, Carlisle, Bella and Angela. However mistaken he might be thought to be about eternity and his soul, he is principled and compassionate as he seeks to do the best for one he loves. He allows for wisdom in his life from others and is prepared to make peace with Jacob, despite the active competition between them for Bella's affections. His willingness to go against the grain of his vampire nature and to respect human beings is a positive attribute, even before we begin to fully understand the wider character that he portrays throughout the pages of the *Twilight Saga*.

FREE WILL

Much as we might admire the principled but fallible Edward, we need to address a key contradiction at the heart of his understanding of life and that of several other characters. If there is a weakness in the premise of the entire series, the issue we are about to address captures it. It gravitates around the tension between free will and predestination.

The entire series is introduced by a verse from Genesis:

> *but you must not eat from the tree of the knowledge of good and evil, for when you eat of it you will surely die.*
>
> GENESIS 2:17

This key scripture marks the moment when it becomes clear that men and women have free will, but that there will be consequences with respect to the choice that we make. Is the apple on the cover of *Twilight* a symbolic reference to the fruit that was seductively offered to men and women by the ancient serpent? Or is Meyer simply suggesting the possibility of free will and asking how we might use it?

Meyer has made it clear in interviews that she believes that part of the function of the story is to explore ideas about free will. In an interview with Lev Grossman of *Time* magazine, she said: 'We have free will, which is a huge gift from God.' Reflecting on how

Edward controls his blood lust, she comments: 'I really think that's the underlying metaphor of my vampires. It doesn't matter where you're stuck in life or what you think you have to do; you can always choose something else. There's always a different path.'

The decision to abstain from humans is the huge symbolic act of free will that stands at the heart of the story. Although their vampire state is described as 'a destiny none of us wanted', this is more likely to refer to the realities of their present state rather than to signify that such an event was predestined by a higher power. Indeed, Edward says very clearly at this point that he can choose to rise above and conquer the boundaries of his destiny.

Carlisle and those who emulate him are saying that they will go against their nature to pursue good. Edward verbalizes this in *Midnight Sun*: 'I didn't have to go to her home. I didn't have to kill her. Obviously, I was a rational, thinking creature, and I had a choice. There was always a choice.'

The scope of that free will is widened by the treatment of Alice's gift of foreseeing the future. Alice tells us that 'the future is not set in stone' and that the decisions people make when they change their minds can mean that 'the whole future shifts'.

The fiery vampire Garrett rallies those who support the Cullen family with the accusation that the Volturi, in trying to precipitate a conflict, are seeking the death of their free will, their ability to choose not to kill and the influence that has on others.

Edward reinforces the free will concept and opens up the nature-versus-nurture debate among the vampires even further when he explains how Jasper is coming to terms with the possibility that Bella may already have exercised significant self-control even in her early weeks of vampirehood:

> *He's wondering if the newborn madness is really as difficult as we've always thought, or if, with the right focus and attitude, anyone could do as well as Bella. Even now — perhaps he only had such difficulty because he believes it is natural and unavoidable. Maybe if he expected more of himself, he would rise to those expectations. You're making him question a lot of deep-rooted assumptions, Bella.*

So far, so good. But there is a problem. Many of the characters also speak of fate, destiny and the irresistible will of an unseen rule.

While the vampires exercise their free will

by resisting human blood, it would seem that the werewolves don't have quite the same opportunities. When the vampires are active near their territory there is an involuntary initiation of the young Indian men into a new wolf identity. Within this wolf identity they will find themselves captive to an 'imprinting' rule that means that at some point they will meet their future wife and there will be no choice – they will be utterly compelled and indeed happy to form this new relationship.

We also find the language of destiny in the mouths of those who believe that the future can be changed by our choices. Edward talks of a 'mismanaged destiny' that causes him to be the nearest available 'protector' for the vulnerable Bella. Is he 'fighting fate' in his attempts to keep her from harm? Bella also ponders whether her 'number is up' and whether his rescue attempts are 'interfering with fate'.

Carlisle also identifies a hidden hand at work in the relationship between Edward and Bella. Perhaps, he reflects, there is a higher purpose, perhaps it was meant to be. Bella is not seen as a character who engages in rational choice about her relationship with Edward. She wonders if there was a choice, really. She confesses: 'My decision was made, made before I'd ever consciously chosen.'

The inner contradiction in the narrative between fate, destiny or predestination and personal free will does not easily resolve itself. In the background of ideas about fate are the perceived actions of a higher power at work in the life of the individual. Most would understand free will to include the ability to change our situation by making rational choices and exercising our will.

Within the context of the *Twilight Saga*, much of the talk of fate and destiny occurs during highly emotional speeches by key characters. The more reflective speech about choice seems to occur more in the context of discussion or quiet reflection. One indicates the debate that may constantly exercise our minds, the other the reality of how we will actually live and act.

The argument will not be an academic one for many who read these books. Those operating within a Christian context will be aware that there are two schools of thought that dominate the debate.

One group lays very little emphasis on man's ability to make good choices and would seem to infer that much of our life has been planned for us by God. We are to try to find out what the plan is and be prepared for the fact that he allows the bad stuff that happens to us to help us grow to maturity.

Alternatively, significant numbers of people

within orthodox Christianity believe that God is at work, both in history and in our lives, but that we must make choices with respect to following him and seek his aid on the journey that he has invited us to take part in. They do not believe our future is fixed but understand that the one who breathed stars into space is more than capable of anticipating our decisions and continuing to interact with us and others as he moves towards his eternal goals. They believe that when bad things happen, it is often because of fallen humanity and that such experiences have not been sent to test our mettle as part of the will of God.

The short paragraphs above cannot begin to do justice to a debate that spans the centuries and occupies the minds of scholars around the world to this present day. But in this context they frame the issues.

Stephenie Meyer has set the debate about free will in a narrative where the key characters must choose to resist an impulse that is intrinsic to their nature. Given the nature of the storyline, she cannot supply all the additional advice, wisdom and reflection on the role of the Holy Spirit that would characterize a Christian perspective on the subject. But in a culture where personal responsibility is often marginalized by voices that say we have the right to follow our impulses, her raising of the subject is welcome.

IS THE *TWILIGHT SAGA* GOOD NEWS?

The word 'gospel' finds its root meaning in the idea of 'good news'. Is the *Twilight* 'gospel' good news? Maybe we should step back and take one final look at how the books approach the subject of right and wrong, good and evil.

It's in the nature of the moral epic tradition, within which these books stand, that there should be some clearly identifiable 'bad' people with whom readers will not bond. Having emotionally identified with those on the side of humanity and decency, the reader is then invited to identify in different ways with the key characters and their strengths and weaknesses.

The language of morality is never far from the lips of our storytellers in these tales. Alice hints at moral complexity when urging Edward not to leave as he becomes overwhelmed with the difficulties surrounding a relationship with Bella. 'There are many right ways, and many wrong ways, though, aren't there?' she tells him. Bella teases him for being such a moral vampire and is very clear that although he may be dangerous, he is not bad.

Edward mentally wrestles with himself, knowing that his restraint with Bella is both right, moral and ethical – but not what he actually really wants. As he reflects on why there may be no heaven for him, he ponders on the rules that must govern life and quotes from the biblical Ten Commandments.

Alice and Jasper, we discover, developed a conscience and moved away from hunting humans without outside guidance, and came to Carlisle seeking like-minded people. The astonishing Benjamin, who appears in the final chapters of the saga with remarkable miracle-working powers, is said to have a highly developed sense of right and wrong.

Moral thinking will result in moral choice. A large-scale story like the *Twilight Saga* will have characters who are instinctively good, others whom we sympathize with but are imperfect, and yet others who are resolutely evil.

If we now take the moral temperature of the story, will we find a healthy patient?

FORGIVENESS

This is a quality exhibited by Bella towards both Jacob and Edward. When she is in danger of turning her back on forgiveness, Charlie Swan provokes her to keep forgiving. Edward seeks forgiveness from Bella and the Volturi overlord Aro asks for forgiveness as he and his tribe retreat from the confrontation provoked by Irena.

LOVING YOUR NEIGHBOUR

Not if he's spotty Eric, it would seem. But that incident apart, several of the characters exhibit a selfless concern for others. The one singled out as embodying unconditional love for others is Angela Weber, who avoids the hypocrisy and shallowness attributed to several of her school colleagues.

VIOLENCE

Carlisle exemplifies an approach to life which seeks to respect the humanity and dignity of others. He will attempt to defuse violent situations and will only mandate self-defence. He has a reverence for life which others seek to follow. It is perhaps typical of Bella's amoral approach to life that she decides that Jacob will be her best friend, whether he kills people or not in his new wolf identity. She always appears to be thinking with her feelings.

SACRIFICE

Bella is deeply moved by the Quileute story of the third wife of their great warrior chief. She cut herself during a battle in order to distract a vampire attacker and enable the survival of others. Bella attempts to do the same thing during the epic battle in the clearing with the murderous Victoria.

THE UNBORN

Stephenie Meyer invites debate about the status of the unborn child when it becomes clear that Bella is pregnant with a very rapidly growing and unusual child. Edward describes the child in the womb as a 'thing'. Jacob refers to 'it'. Edward uses the term 'fetus' in conversation, but Jacob suspects he is being polite, rather than speaking his mind.

Bella returns again and again to her feeling of connectedness with the child living inside her. In the aftermath of the birth, it is clear that Renesmee has had formative experiences while still in the womb, including her sensing of the connectedness between Jacob and Bella.

The perception that Meyer was taking a pro-life (i.e. anti-abortion) stance caused some readers to reject the *Breaking Dawn* book. Going ahead with the birth was justified within the book, despite genuine fears that the mother might die (grounds for an abortion in some religious traditions), by using the deeply ironic defence that they had to respect Bella's choice.

MONEY

Bella and Angela emerge with some credit as they do not make money and the trappings of wealth key to their identity. As we have seen, Alice leads the way in enthusiastic consumerism.

SEX

Well, there's lots of it. It just doesn't involve actual intercourse until Bella and Edward are married. We are sold the beauty myth of Western culture alongside the depiction of Edward as a sex object. Our heroine has no real ideology in this area: she simply lives on her feelings.

POWER

Two spiritualities are presented to us. One is the mythical and fantastic lore of the Quileute, the other a form of personal spiritual power emanating from the mind. For many Western readers the Native American myths are too fantastic to be anything other than a story. The mind-power spirituality, however, will find a deep echo in another blockbuster, Dan Brown's *The Lost Symbol*. It offers a religion without ritual or commitment and crucially, without limits, and the power that many crave in order to control their circumstances.

SHARDS OF WISDOM

We are ever mindful that we are not perfect. Like the apostle Paul, we understand that sometimes we do that which we do not wish to do and fail to do that which we should (Romans 7). So as we take the moral temperature of these best-selling books, we would do well to do so with humility.

There are shards of wisdom scattered throughout these books. We find women who unconditionally love. We discover a man dedicated to peace. We find people willing to forgive and to sacrifice for others. We discover a worldwide clan of people who will work to control their destructive impulses. We find a family who will nurture wisdom.

We find God or an echo of him. We didn't expect to find Jesus or the Holy Spirit, but without them we find Edward trapped in a world where he can't find grace or forgiveness.

At the heart of the book we find the idols of beauty, occult power, consumerism and undisciplined eroticism paraded with a degree of naivety in some cases and with unthinking relish in others.

Yet the *Twilight Saga* has much to admire. Apart from anything else, the books are an excellent read, and there is much in them that is wholesome and good. But the flaws are serious, and the series should be read with caution and thought. I hope that this short book has helped this process, because to read uncritically is always dangerous. Obviously the *Twilight Saga* is not the bible of a new religion – which is just as well, for if it were, then you would have to say it offers a false gospel. Enjoy, but do not believe.

There are four books which will help you discover the real gospel, if you haven't already. They are packaged with some others and they've sold a lot more than 70 million. Go to www.biblegateway.com and search for Matthew, Mark, Luke and John. You'll find epic tales of love, counter-cultural compassion, political defiance, simple living and a humble spiritual power.

NOTES AND SOURCES

For ease of reading, I have not footnoted the chapters of this book. With the large amount of descriptive detail covered by this analysis, it would have been visually distracting. The notes below refer to the books and page numbers that the analysis has been drawn from. This list is thorough but not exhaustive.

PUBLISHING INFORMATION

Twilight: Atom Books. 2009 edition. ISBN: 9781904233657
New Moon: Atom Books. 2009 edition. ISBN: 978904233886
Eclipse: Atom Books. A 2009 edition. ISBN: 978904233916
Breaking Dawn: Atom Books. 2009 edition.
ISBN: 978905654284 (Hardback)
Midnight Sun: www.stepheniemeyer.com

CHAPTER 1: THE USES OF ENCHANTMENT

The summaries in this chapter draw from all five books:
Twilight, *New Moon*, *Eclipse*, *Breaking Dawn* and *Midnight Sun*.

CHAPTER 2: THE FEAR OF THE DEAD

Two key books with respect to the background information in this chapter were: *From Demons to Dracula: The Creation of the Modern Vampire Myth* by Matthew Beresford (Reaktion Books, London, 2008) and *The Lure of the Vampire: Gender, Fiction and Fandom from Bram Stoker to Buffy* by Milly Williamson (Wallflower Press, London, 2005). The other summaries in this chapter draw from all five *Twilight Saga* books.

CHAPTER 3: YOU'VE GOT TO BE PERFECT

Twilight pages 17, 23, 26, 37, 38, 41, 43, 52, 61, 63, 64, 67, 69, 74, 93, 96, 100, 104, 119, 167, 173, 179, 184, 186, 192, 193, 200, 210, 213, 214, 221, 224, 225, 255, 300, 313, 424.
New Moon pages 11, 20, 62, 95, 164, 389, 413.
Eclipse pages 8, 121, 46, 113, 145, 147.
Breaking Dawn pages 39, 222, 372, 373, 374.
Midnight Sun pages 102, 103, 146.

CHAPTER 4: MAKE ME LIKE ALICE

Twilight pages 71, 188, 302, 320.
New Moon pages 9, 22, 134, 138.
Eclipse pages 130, 556.
Breaking Dawn pages 41, 44, 47, 65, 75, 160, 368, 378, 442, 484.
Midnight Sun pages 238, 244, 255.

CHAPTER 5: SEX AND THE COUNTRY

Twilight pages 77, 164, 157, 168, 175, 183, 188, 190, 191, 192, 193, 197, 202, 211, 239, 242, 243, 247, 261, 271, 317.
New Moon pages 2, 15, 45, 46, 273, 325, 329, 330, 365, 451, 452.
Eclipse pages 53, 74, 100, 116, 166, 167, 171, 293, 392, 396, 397–399, 401, 468, 475, 536, 547, 549.

Breaking Dawn pages 23, 76, 364, 388, 394, 446, 488.
Midnight Sun pages 211, 220, 235, 250.

CHAPTER 6: THE OCCULT STING IN THE TALE

Twilight pages 157, 233, 253, 268, 269, 330.
New Moon page 256.
Eclipse page 83.
Breaking Dawn pages 513–699.

CHAPTER 7: IS THERE HOPE FOR MY SOUL?

Twilight pages 207, 236, 269.
New Moon pages 61, 457, 477.
Eclipse pages 482, 549.
Breaking Dawn pages 402, 430, 656, 666.
Midnight Sun pages 80, 90, 218.

CHAPTER 8: TWILIGHT OF THE SOUL

Twilight pages 75, 152, 267.
New Moon pages 32, 33, 80, 120, 253, 265, 283, 376, 380.
Eclipse pages 106, 175, 209, 402, 472–3, 475, 478, 525.
Breaking Dawn pages 120, 163, 174, 216, 220, 556, 607, 686.
Midnight Sun pages 17, 55, 79, 82, 83, 192, 209, 215, 226.

EVERYONE'S TALKING ABOUT IT, SHOULDN'T YOU BE?

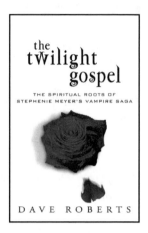

IF YOU ENJOYED THE BOOK ...

WHY NOT JOIN THE DEBATE?

www.facebook.com/thetwilightgospel

I have set up a Facebook Profile where I can post events and interact online. I'd love to hear your thoughts and feelings about the book and about the *Twilight Saga*.

The forum will also provide an opportunity for you to interact with others and share your concerns and experiences.

Thanks for reading, see you online.

Dave Roberts